MAPPING WOODY GUTHRIE

MAPPING
WOODY GUTHRIE

WILL KAUFMAN

UNIVERSITY OF OKLAHOMA PRESS : NORMAN

This book is published with the generous assistance
of the Wallace C. Thompson Endowment Fund,
University of Oklahoma Foundation.

LIBRARY OF CONGRESS CATALOGING-IN-PUBLICATION DATA

Names: Kaufman, Will, author.
Title: Mapping Woody Guthrie / Will Kaufman.
Description: Norman : University of Oklahoma Press, [2018] | Series: American
  popular music series ; Volume 4 | Includes bibliographical references and index.
Identifiers: LCCN 2018024136 | ISBN 978-0-8061-6178-5 (hardcover : alk. paper)
Subjects: LCSH: Guthrie, Woody, 1912–1967. | Folk singers—United States—
  Biography.
Classification: LCC ML410.G978 K37 2018 | DDC 782.42162/130092 [B] —dc23
  LC record available at https://lccn.loc.gov/2018024136

Mapping Woody Guthrie is Volume 4 in the American Popular Music Series.

The paper in this book meets the guidelines for permanence and durability of the
Committee on Production Guidelines for Book Longevity of the Council on Library
Resources, Inc. ∞

For Ron Cohen

CONTENTS

ILLUSTRATIONS

PREFACE

"This Land Is Your Land" doesn't count, if anyone asks me where and when my interest in Woody Guthrie really began. Everyone knew that song when I was growing up in Montclair, New Jersey, in the 1960s. Just like the little kids who "pledged allegiance to the wall" in Simon and Garfunkel's nostalgic ode "My Little Town," we often sang "This Land Is Your Land" robotically to the classroom wall on the heels of our equally robotic Pledge of Allegiance. With the pledge, some of us actually didn't know if our "one nation under God" was meant to be "indivisible" or "invisible"—such was the way we mumbled through it. With "This Land," we droned tunelessly about someone wandering beneath an "endless skyway." We had a hard time imagining what this "skyway" was meant to look like. Did it look anything like the Pulaski Skyway, the massive black girder-and-concrete highway that lifted us over the Jersey swamps on the drive into New York City? Nor, back then, did we have any idea what "dust clouds" were or why they should have been "rolling" anywhere. Maybe if we'd grown up in Oklahoma, we'd have had a better idea. Or maybe if we'd grown up in the thirties—even in New Jersey, where, back then, they certainly knew about the Dust Bowl ravaging the prairie states to the west.

Some of us, myself included, at least knew that "This Land" was written by Woody Guthrie. In my case, that had a lot to do with the family into which I was born. My parents had Pete Seeger and the Weavers' records lying around the house, and my older brother had the two-album recording of the Hollywood Bowl and Carnegie Hall memorial concerts produced shortly after Guthrie's death. This was my introduction to Guthrie outside of "This Land Is Your Land." So I sometimes heard the voices of Will Geer, Robert Ryan, and Peter Fonda drifting down the stairs from my brother's attic bedroom—they were reciting some of Guthrie's poetry and prose. Or I'd hear the singing of Joan Baez, Richie Havens, Bob Dylan, Odetta, Ramblin' Jack Elliott, Judy Collins, Tom Paxton, and Pete Seeger. I had no idea if any of them sounded at all like the guy who actually wrote the songs. (Only much later did I find out that the one who probably came the closest was Ramblin' Jack.) So there were still a number of degrees of separation between the source and me—too many, for a while, for my interest to be piqued.

This all changed when I heard Ry Cooder's mesmeric slide guitar version of Guthrie's "Vigilante Man" about the time I turned twenty. Even then, I didn't realize how "deterritorialized" (to borrow Edward Comentale's phrase) was Cooder's rendition—how far it had drifted from the "regional coordinates" of the Dust Bowl migration plotted into Guthrie's original.[1] Unlike anyone else, Cooder had recorded it as a slow Delta bottleneck blues, invoking more of Blind Willie Johnson than Woody Guthrie. It was as though the song had been lifted out of the California Hoovervilles of the thirties and dragged through the streets of the sundown towns of the Jim Crow South. This was the moment I seriously began "Thinking of Woody Guthrie" (to quote Country Joe McDonald's album of the same title) in sociopolitical terms.[2] But still, I was no closer to Guthrie himself—no closer to the source.

By the time I thought to go to the source, I was no longer living in America. I was in England, doing what many American expatriates from Washington Irving onward had been doing: studying and writing about home from a foreign perspective. The physical distance seemed to enable a corresponding critical distance—a cooler edge somewhat removed from the infection of knee-jerk patriotism or blind cultural celebration. My PhD in American literature came from the University of Wales in Aberystwyth. I taught American literature in colleges and universities in Staffordshire, Cheshire, and Lancashire (as well as Indonesia for two years as a volunteer). Mark Twain, Edith Wharton, Henry James, Fitzgerald, Hemingway, Gertrude Stein, T. S. Eliot, and James Baldwin: I was particularly drawn to those writers who had, for whatever reasons, chosen to put some distance between themselves and America in order to interrogate what it means to *be* American.

The expatriate experience can sometimes be difficult, especially when you are not at one with the prevailing political Zeitgeist at home. The Dixie

Chicks found this out, famously, when they chose to criticize George W. Bush from the stage of a London venue, a little over a week before the US invasion of Iraq in 2003. Much of the wrath they incurred back home came down to the fact that they had uttered their words from a foreign stage. The Dixie Chicks were only visiting England; I lived there. And by 2006, with much of the world's opinion ranged against the United States (and the Tony Blair government) for starting a disastrous war based on a flimsy pretext, if not an outright fabrication (those fabled "weapons of mass destruction"), being an American expatriate was not easy. As I listened to the belligerent and hawkish voices coming out of Washington (as well as the American right-wing media), I again began "thinking of Woody Guthrie" as some kind of antidote. I developed a performance piece on Guthrie that I still take to venues throughout Europe and America—and, as we do when we're trying to get some kind of a performance off the ground, I sought supportive words and endorsements from people who matter.

The first I wrote to was Pete Seeger, who invited me to phone him—legendarily busy as he always was. He asked me, "Are you familiar with the phrase, 'The Other America'?" I replied that yes, I knew of it from Michael Harrington's 1962 study of the same name, which, among other things, argued for the possibilities of democratic socialism in the United States.[3] Well, Woody Guthrie, Seeger said, was the voice of that "other America"—and that voice needed to be broadcast now more than ever.

I do not know if I would ever have thought so hard about Woody Guthrie if I myself hadn't become deterritorialized at that time in global history. I did know—and do know—that place matters, as does time. Once again, as I write this in March 2018, it is a tough time to be an American abroad. Once again, as the world bears witness to some of the ugliest and most hateful manifestations of American xenophobia in living memory, there are those who yearn to hear the voice of some other America. For me, and for many others still, that voice is Woody's voice.

MAPPING WOODY GUTHRIE

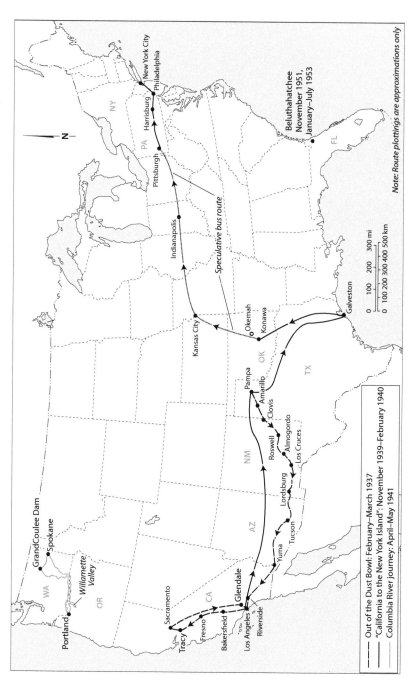

Guthrie's formative US travels

Beluthahatchee
November 1951,
January–July 1953

Note: Route plottings are approximations only

Speculative bus route

New York City
Philadelphia
Harrisburg
Pittsburgh
Indianapolis
Kansas City
Okemah
Konawa
Galveston
Pampa
Amarillo
Clovis
Roswell
Almogordo
Los Cruces
Lordsburg
Tucson
Yuma
Glendale
Los Angeles
Riverside
Bakersfield
Fresno
Tracy
Sacramento
Grand Coulee Dam
Spokane
Portland
Willamette Valley

NY
PA
FL
OK
TX
NM
AZ
CA
OR
WA

N

0   100   200   300 mi
0 100 200 300 400 500 km

—·—·— Out of the Dust Bowl: February–March 1937
———— "California to the New York Island": November 1939–February 1940
———— Columbia River journey: April–May 1941

INTRODUCTION
EINSTEIN'S LIGHT RAYS

Why not begin with Einstein? Woody Guthrie idolized "his fellow humanist socialist," and Guthrie family lore even has it that he once made a pilgrimage to Princeton to visit the professor in his laboratory.[1] This was roughly forty-five years after Einstein had established the interdependence of time and space (a theory further refined by his teacher, Hermann Minkowski, who concluded that "space by itself, and time by itself, are doomed to fade away into mere shadows, and only a kind of union of the two will preserve an independent reality").[2] Thus, any study of Guthrie's relation to place will have to take into account his relation to time, the "when" being as important as the "where."

Einstein had proved—in Guthrie's words—that after a light ray "hits the old trail called time" it eventually "comes back, a little bit bent up maybe, but better bent than to just not have no light ray at all."[3] This might be a good analogy for Guthrie on his own wanderings, criss-crossing America and the high seas, with the inevitable wear and tear on his body compounded by the increasing depredations of Huntington's disease, and with the American body politic itself buffeted by economic depression, war, Jim Crow racism, and political upheavals of all kinds. Who or what could sustain that kind of weathering without coming out of it "a little bit bent up"?

Guthrie seized on Einstein's theory of relativity to craft an imaginative political viewpoint fully in keeping with their shared identity of "humanist socialist." Not only was the earth "like a little rubber ball" in space, with no "east north south nor west," but there was "no sucha place as you could call

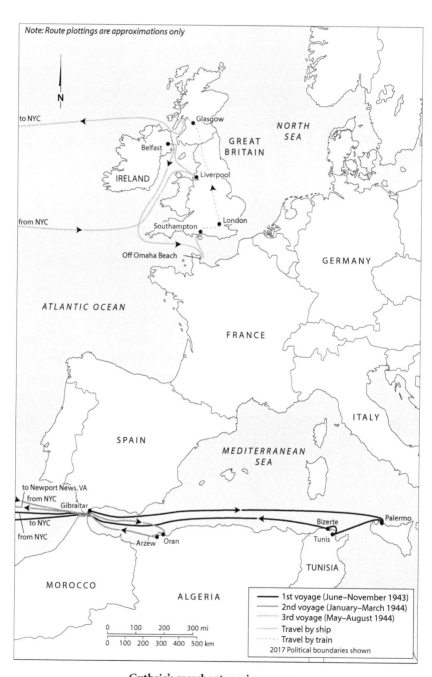

Guthrie's merchant marine voyages

up nor call down. No such a place as high nor low. Course you can see for your own eyes how this is the finest thing that's ever been proved since any of us jumped out of the bag. Us low folks don't have to look up to you high ones no longer starting out from here and now."[4]

This is all very well in theoretical terms, but of course, in history, the confluence of time and space (or place) *does* matter. Consider the implications of David King Dunaway's observation about one particular day in one particular place: March 3, 1940, in New York City, when (and where) Guthrie met Pete Seeger and Lead Belly. "By themselves, these three could not have moved American musical history," Dunaway writes. "But their tastes coincided with the New Deal's radical patriotism and folklore activities. . . . This *was* a movement, the All-American Left-Wing Folk Song Revival Movement."[5] Were it not for the fortuitous meeting of time and place, there would have been no equally fortuitous meeting between these three giants of American folk music history, who themselves had been born at just the right time to make such an impact.

Even before that fateful meeting in New York City, time and place had been visibly controlling forces in the making of Woody Guthrie as an individual and as an artist. He was born, he said, "in the hungriest/richest of states"—Oklahoma—in 1912, with the abundant oil beneath the surface still "a whisper in the dark, a rumor, a gamble."[6] Politically, something important was happening in Oklahoma in 1912. It was where and when "the socialist tide was rising," as Milton Cantor wrote, placing Guthrie's Oklahoma at the heart of the agrarian radicalism through which Eugene Debs had become "the hero and symbol of socialism in America . . . [opposing] capitalism since it was 'inherently unjust, inhuman, unintelligent'"—a homegrown brand of radicalism embodying "the unity of populist, Marxist, militant trade union, and Judeo-Christian traditions." In the year of Guthrie's birth, the greatest electoral gains for Debs's Socialist Party—of anywhere in America—were to be had in Oklahoma.[7] So socialism was in the air of Woody Guthrie's home state, and its overtones were still reverberating when the oil was finally discovered near Guthrie's birthplace, Okemah, in 1920, transforming the measured passage of rural time into the mad rush of the boomtown. As Guthrie recalled,

There's all kinds of guys that hit town—you just wake up one morning and they're *there*. You don't know where they come from—there's fifteen or twenty thousand of 'em out there in a little town that used to be five or six hundred. Farming people are sort of slow, poking around, you know, going to the mail box and back, take an hour to tell you a story about something. But all at once here are fifteen or twenty thousand guys arrived on the street out there. . . . Everybody is one big army—transient workers. They're gonna work out from there a few months or a few years at most, and be gone. They don't even build houses, they don't build homes, they don't put down foundations—they put up a little boxcar house that costs twenty-five or thirty dollars apiece, and move on as quick as the oil well's drilled.[8]

One of Guthrie's early songs, written in 1935 when he was all of twenty-three—long after the oil had dried up and the socialist tide had crested—reflects the experience of that formative time and place and the hold it still had on his imagination. The song, "If I Was Everything on Earth," carries the embryonic hallmarks of the socialism that had somehow worked its way into his consciousness while he was still a small child: he would "turn out all the prisoners / And put in all the rich"; or "make the groceries free" and "pass out suits of clothing / At least three times a week."[9]

Then, in the wake of the socialist whirlwind and the oil busts in Oklahoma and Texas, came the dust storms, turning out a wandering tribe of American refugees numbering close to half a million, transforming the nation's demographic and cultural landscapes as comprehensively as its natural one. In the mix was Woody Guthrie, making his way westward toward California's Eden, gathering on the road and the rails the store of knowledge underpinning a body of writing that would catapult him to international renown. As Guthrie implied during a live concert, it was the coincidence of time and place that had presented him with such a unique creative possibility: "I just happened to be *in* the Dust Bowl. I mean, it wasn't something that I particularly wanted or craved, but since I was there and the dust was there, I thought, well, I'll write a little song about it."[10] Of course, he wrote more than just "a little song." In his *Dust Bowl Ballads* (1940), Guthrie did for the

Dust Bowl migrants what John Steinbeck did for them in literature—in *The Grapes of Wrath*—and what photographers like Dorothea Lange and Arthur Rothstein did for them through the still image. He dignified them, fought for them, gave them a story and a voice. Some would argue that in so doing, he became the father of the modern American protest song. Nearly sixty years after the album's release, in the notes to one of several reissues, Dave Marsh nailed down the importance of Guthrie and his *Dust Bowl Ballads*:

> He set a standard to which many of today's best songwriters still aspire. Like Dylan, Springsteen and KRS-One (who stands in the line of great talking bluesmen), he gave his listeners stories and characters that help them better understand themselves. So these songs are not only historical, they are history itself, history being that which links present to future. That is why, sixty years after they were recorded, Woody Guthrie's *Dust Bowl Ballads* still deserve their place among the greatest American stories and songs.[11]

After his experiences in the Dust Bowl and on the road—and, it must be said, with his first wife and three children largely marginalized—Guthrie was ripe for more formative input once in California. Again, the coincidences of time and place had their impact. Guthrie had hoped simply to become a country music singer on the radio, but meeting the socialist activist Ed Robbin on the Los Angeles radio station KFVD brought Guthrie into a whole new political milieu peopled by the likes of J. Frank Burke, Will Geer, Al Richmond, and John Steinbeck, who became to varying degrees his patrons and mentors. Through his KFVD position, Guthrie was commissioned to report on the conditions in the Californian migrant camps, as well as in jails and on picket lines, where the outlines of his political activism began to take shape.

In the backdrop of everything local was the confluence of national and international crises. The Depression, the Dust Bowl, the New Deal, the growth of European fascism and Nazism, the Spanish Civil War, the Hitler-Stalin Pact, the onset of the Second World War, and Guthrie's own sojourn in California all took place during one of the most tempestuous decades in American political and cultural history, what historian Michael Denning has called the "age of the CIO" (Congress of Industrial Organizations), the period that "marked the first time in the history of the United States that the left—the tradition of radical democratic movements for social transforma-tion—had a central, indeed shaping, impact on American culture."[12] Of all these movements for social and political "transformation," the one in which Guthrie was the most deeply immersed in his California years was the Pop-ular Front, "the insurgent social movement forged from the labor militancy of the fledgling CIO, the anti-fascist solidarity with Spain, Ethiopia, China, and the refugees from Hitler, and the political struggles on the left wing of the New Deal. . . . [C]oinciding with the Communist Party's period of greatest influence in US society, the Popular Front became a radical histor-ical bloc uniting industrial unionists, Communists, independent socialists, community activists, and émigré anti-fascists."[13]

Guthrie enjoyed playing with the knee-jerk association between his Pop-ular Front activism and the bugbear of communist subversion, declaring in one wartime autobiographical fragment, "Well, boys, I don't even know what a communist is. I never did see one to know him. . . . And as far as the 'communist' goes, I'm going to go and look till I find out what they are, and I'm going to join up with them and be one of them for the rest of my life!"[14] There is no documentary evidence that Guthrie ever did officially "join up with them and be one of them," but he certainly did "see one to know him"—many, in fact, with whom he worked closely.

It could hardly have been otherwise, given that he was a folk musician at that time and in not one but two significant places: first Los Angeles, where the Popular Front maintained its greatest cultural and industrial strength of anywhere on the West Coast, and New York, where the same held true for the East Coast. Although Guthrie wrote prose and dabbled at the peripheries of the film industry and live theater, it was as a folk musician that he was best placed to forge an identity in keeping with the currents of the Popular Front. As Robbie Lieberman points out, "The most important and lasting effect of the Popular Front in the cultural realm was the identification of 'the folk' with left-wing politics. . . . Though expressed in literature, film, and drama, this unity was nowhere more apparent than in the songs that began to be created and disseminated during the period."[15]

By the time of Guthrie's arrival in New York in 1940, all the ground-work had been done for the city's unrivaled claim to proprietorship of the

American folk music renaissance that would begin with his first encounter with Pete Seeger and Lead Belly. Once again, timing was everything. For the previous decade, music of a self-consciously proletarian or progressive stamp had been dominated, for the most part, by "revolutionary" workers' choruses singing semiclassical art songs in a variety of European languages (due to their origins in urban immigrant communities). Some of the most prominent composers and choral leaders were to be found in the New York–based Composers' Collective, comprising graduates from the country's top music conservatories—musicians such as Elie Siegmeister, Jacob Schaefer, Earl Robinson, Lan Adomian, and Charles Seeger (father of Pete). Their aesthetic and spiritual guru was the German modernist composer Hanns Eisler, who "demanded that songs be both politically and musically progressive. In the words of Charles Seeger, proletarian music was defined by its militance in text and tune. . . . It was to be revolutionary in content and nationalist in form."[16] It was so dissonant, so strident and modernist, that very few American workers cared to listen to it, let alone sing it. As a leading communist writer, Mike Gold, asked in exasperation, "Why don't American workers sing?"[17]

In fact, American workers *were* singing—for instance, in the textile mills of Gastonia, North Carolina, where the likes of Ella May Wiggins had been singing such handcrafted songs as "A Mill Mother's Lament" for the struggling National Textile Workers Union (before she was murdered in 1929). New York activists knew nothing about her until Margaret Larkin published her songs in the *Nation* and *New Masses*. Workers were also singing in the coalfields of "Bloody Harlan," Kentucky, where Florence Reece sang her anthem, "Which Side Are You On?" for the fledgling, embattled National Miners Union. At the same time and in the same place, Aunt Molly Jackson was singing "Ragged Hungry Blues" and "I Am a Union Woman." But no one in New York knew about them until a committee of writers led by Theodore Dreiser returned from Harlan with Jackson and her half-brother and fellow songwriter Jim Garland in tow. The West Virginia activist-musicians Ray and Lita Auville were singing loudly enough over their guitar and fiddle, but no one in New York heard them until Gold had championed them in the *Daily Worker*. Meanwhile, in various workers' colleges, North and South, labor activists were using and refashioning African American spirituals and other folk songs as organizing tools. Out of the Highlander Folk School in eastern Tennessee, under the musical stewardship of Zilphia Horton, came "We Will Overcome," later brought to New York by Pete Seeger, who subsequently transformed it into the civil rights anthem "We Shall Overcome." Organizers from the Brookwood Labor School in Katonah, New York, went to the coalfields of West Virginia and came back with the spiritual "We Shall Not Be Moved" as sung by members of the miners' union. From the Commonwealth Labor College in Arkansas came Lee Hays, who would later sing with Guthrie and Seeger in the Almanac Singers, and who brought with him scores of songs he had learned both at Commonwealth and at Highlander before it.[18]

Gradually, as the Americanizing mission of the Popular Front began to take hold, the leading cultural arbiters both within and outside the communist movement began to pay more attention to folk music in the service of labor activism and the proletarianization of American culture. Even the members of the Composers' Collective, having previously derided folk music as an apolitical or reactionary art form, climbed on board, working more and more American folk sources into their compositions. By 1939 the Communist Party's Writers' Congress would have on its panels the likes of Aunt Molly Jackson, the folklorist Benjamin A. Botkin, the composer Earl Robinson, and—perhaps the most important single individual in the developing folk music renaissance—Alan Lomax, in charge of the Archive of American Folk Song at the Library of Congress. The party's leading magazine, *New Masses,* published the song collector Lawrence Gellert's series of articles that would form the basis of his two comprehensive volumes, *Negro Songs of Protest* (1936) and *Me and My Captain* (1939).[19] In Washington, DC, with the Roosevelt administration sponsoring a number of folk preservation projects under the Works Progress Administration, Charles Seeger—now thoroughly committed to the propagation of folk music—presided, with Benjamin Botkin, over a sweeping program of fieldwork and recording, relying upon the efforts of such folk song collectors as John and Alan Lomax, Stetson Kennedy, Mary E. Barnacle, and Margaret Valiant, among many others.[20]

Of all these folk song collectors and activists, it was Alan Lomax who would be the most instrumental in driving Woody Guthrie into the public consciousness. He had many friends in high places, whether it was the Roosevelt administration, the broadcasting industry, or the recording industry. Folk music historian Richard Reuss argues that "it is not inappropriate to call the ardent activist folk singers of the Popular Front era the 'Lomax singers'"—such was Lomax's influence in establishing and furthering the musical careers of Guthrie, Pete Seeger, Lead Belly, Josh White, Sonny Terry and Brownie McGhee, Burl Ives, Jelly Roll Morton, the Golden Gate Quartet, and others.[21] It was Lomax who (along with Will Geer) introduced Guthrie to Seeger and Lead Belly; it was Lomax who first recorded Guthrie for the Library of Congress; and it was Lomax who secured Guthrie's first commercial recording contract with RCA Victor, out of which came *Dust Bowl Ballads*. Moreover, when officials at the Bonneville Power Administration in the Pacific Northwest wanted a folksinger to write and sing the praises of the Grand Coulee Dam for the public boosting of the New Deal's rural electrification projects, it was Lomax who sent them Woody Guthrie.

There is no telling for sure whether Guthrie would have seen California if it weren't for the Dust Bowl, whether he would have gone to New York were it not for losing his job on KFVD over the Hitler-Stalin Pact, whether he would have seen the Pacific Northwest were it not for a bureaucrat's phone call to Alan Lomax, or whether he would ever have gone to sea were it not for the threat of wartime army induction. But because of these events at these times and in their association with certain places (or spaces), we have the enormous body of Guthrie's songs, prose, poems, and artwork to enrich us.

This book is an attempt to make sense of the confluence of time and space in the making of Woody Guthrie as an artist of enduring influence and significance. I have learned through writing two previous books— *Woody Guthrie, American Radical* (2011) and *Woody Guthrie's Modern World Blues* (2017)—that such an expansive life as his cannot possibly be contained within the covers of one book; nor can a single study do justice to the myriad historical and cultural contexts that must be explored in order to make sense of his artistry. In my case, it took an entire book to examine Guthrie's political awakening and the artistic journey that followed it. It took another to examine his surprising engagements with the phenomena of modernity. Now, once again, a new thread emerges, inviting further exploration: the impact of *where* and *when* on Guthrie's consciousness. This book is an attempt, literally, to map the development of Woody Guthrie as an artist and thinker.

The first chapter, "Dust Bowl Blues," places Guthrie in both his native Oklahoma and the Texas of his young manhood, where the great historical calamity of the Dust Bowl (and arguably the greater calamity of the Great Depression behind it) engendered in him a mode of artistic response that balanced humor with a steely contempt for the threat of annihilation. In chapter 2, "I Ain't Got No Home," the formative place is the road, the migrant trail westward where incredulity and anger merged to inspire in Guthrie an outlaw poetics in response to an inverted social and economic order that appeared to equate homelessness with criminality, and theft with the rule of law. With California as the locus of chapter 3, we see Guthrie drawn into the world of the Popular Front and the communist movement, writing songs speaking of resistance to terror and reflecting his developing bardic persona—the balladeer who could sing because, like Walt Whitman eight decades earlier, he had learned to adopt the voice of the distressed and the dispossessed. Whitman had sung onto the pages of *Leaves of Grass* (1855): "I am the man. . . . I suffered. . . . I was there" (even if he wasn't).[22] Guthrie, too, "was there"—both as witness and as bard—but his bardic "presence," as we shall see, raises a host of problems in terms of history and authenticity.

Chapter 4, "Pastures of Plenty," explores the importance of the Pacific Northwest in Guthrie's writing. Above the gorge of the Columbia River he wrote twenty-six songs in the space of a month, a corpus of conflicted impressions: awe for the grandeur of the natural landscape that would be irrevocably changed—and threatened—by the massive dam-building project that he had been hired to eulogize, reverence for the American worker devoted equally to the pursuit of domestic peace and the forging of weapons of war, and a balancing act between the collective socialism and the rugged individualism that he championed both implicitly and explicitly. In chapter 5, "Somewhere at Sea," Guthrie's merchant marine and US Army writings reveal him at his most belligerent in the fight against fascism, but also reflect an expanding worldview based on his firsthand encounters with people and cultures beyond the shores of America. Guthrie's Columbia River and merchant marine sojourns were, to some extent, side trips that he took from the place that became his permanent home: New York City, the subject of chapter 6. It was here that he produced the great bulk of his writing and artwork, here that he experienced, arguably, the greatest cultural diversity in his entire life, here that he was instrumental in launching the American folk music revival of the 1940s–1960s, here that he died, and from here that his works were largely disseminated. But before the virtual immobilization that overtook him in the last decade of his life, he had one more important trip to take: into the heart of the Jim Crow South—the Florida swamplands of Beluthahatchee, where he produced some of his most trenchant and seething criticisms of American racism, a body of work that has only recently begun to attract sustained scholarly attention.

In its entirety this book aims to present a geographically based study of Woody Guthrie, but as those familiar with his biography will perceive, it is not quite faithful to the chronology of his life. There are many other places from which he drifted and to which he returned, yet one cannot chart all of his comings and goings in a study of this length or nature. Indeed, Guthrie's was such a vagabond spirit that we may never know all the places where he actually set foot. So the necessities of selection have prevailed here, in what is, at best, an approximation of Guthrie's wayward path through the times of his short life. These times brought him to the varied places and spaces that he memorialized in his art.

In the end, Guthrie departed life in the same condition as that in which he'd found his beloved country and his world at large: "a little bit bent up maybe," like Einstein's light rays, but with so much still to celebrate, to champion, to change, and to preserve.

1

DUST BOWL BLUES

Woody Guthrie's name is inextricably linked to one of the greatest environmental catastrophes of modern history, the Dust Bowl of the 1930s. In this, as in so many other aspects of American identity, the power of myth is as important as the power of time and place. Yes, the great mass of Dust Bowl migrants streaming into California had been lumped together under the epithet "Okie," as though they all had come from Oklahoma (in fact, only a quarter of them came from there; the majority had come from Texas, Arkansas, Missouri, Kansas, and Colorado). Moreover, popular culture has cast the typical Dust Bowl migrant as an agricultural worker, while in reality the greatest number were blue- or white-collar town and city dwellers; only 12 percent of interviewed migrants cited "farm failure" as the cause of their displacement. The majority of them did not migrate as far as California, but rather moved only to the next town, the next county, or the nearest bordering state.[1] Nonetheless, largely thanks to four cultural enterprises—John Steinbeck's novel *The Grapes of Wrath* (1939); the John Ford film of the same name (1940); the Farm Security Administration (FSA) photographs by Dorothea Lange, Arthur Rothstein, and others (1937–42); and Guthrie's *Dust Bowl Ballads* (1940)—the stoic "Dust Bowl refugee" battling poverty, prejudice, and political oppression in California has become a signature American figure recognized all around the world.

Guthrie's various soubriquets—"th' Dustiest of the Dust Bowlers," "the Dust Bowl Balladeer," "the Okie Bard"—threaten to costume him as one more character out of Steinbeck's novel, the story of the evicted Oklahoma tenant farmers, the Joad family, displaced by the great dust storms of the thirties. Indeed, when the paid informer Hazel Huffman denounced Guthrie as a Communist before the Special Committee on Un-American Activities (the Dies Committee) in 1941, she erroneously described him as "one of the 'Joads,' or migratory workers" from Oklahoma.[2] Guthrie indeed hailed from Oklahoma, but he spent only the first seventeen years of his life there before moving to the Texas Panhandle town of Pampa. The dust storms feature little, if at all, in his Oklahoma biography, as he made clear in his interviews with Alan Lomax for the *Library of Congress Recordings* (recorded 1940; first released 1964):

> John Steinbeck talks about one end of the Dust Bowl, and that's the Oklahoma end of it, and other people talk about the Colorado and the New Mexico end of it. But if you want to find the very big middle of these dust storms, where they get the blackest and thickest—where the wheat grows, the oil flows and the farmer owes—why, you just go to Amarillo, Texas, and you can spit within walking distance around there, and you'll find you a good dust storm to deal with.[3]

Woody Guthrie birthplace, Okemah, Oklahoma. Walter Smalling, photographer. Historic American Buildings Survey, Library of Congress Prints and Photographs Division, Washington, DC (HABS OKLA,54-OKE.V,1-)

On the same recording, Guthrie took the pains to further establish the distance between himself and the popular "Okie" image: "I wasn't in the class that John Steinbeck called 'the Okies' because my dad to start with was worth about thirty-five or forty thousand dollars, and he had everything hunky-dory. Then he started having a little bad luck."[4] Later in the decade, as he looked back at the punditry and the sociological and political handwringing that had followed the Dust Bowl migration crisis and the proliferation of its imagery in news, literature, film, and photography, Guthrie hit out at the crude stereotyping that had ensued:

> My people
> Are not quaint
> They're not colorful
> [. . . . .]
> It makes me sore to hear or to see or to read
> How you big long-haired writers
> Whack away at my people
> Chew and cut and saw away at my people
> Grind and drill and whittle away at them
> Trying to make out like you are their Savior
> Or their way shower
> Or their finder
> Or their discoverer[5]

In spite of such caveats, however, Guthrie was perfectly happy to maintain his associations with Steinbeck, *The Grapes of Wrath*, his native Oklahoma, and the Dust Bowl itself: "Th' Dustiest of the Dust Bowlers" was his own chosen moniker, even emblazoned on his business cards.

All of this is to assert the central place of Oklahoma in Guthrie's identity, even though he was still a teenager when he left the state. One of his most popular songs, one that he in fact never recorded (although his cousin Leon "Jack" Guthrie did record it, mendaciously claiming authorship), was "Oklahoma Hills," adopted in 2001 as the official state folk song.[6] It establishes well enough Guthrie's nostalgia for a place that, in actual fact, was as much a site of familial and financial trauma as a boyhood prairie idyll. His family's house had burned down shortly after it was built; his older sister Clara had died in a coal-oil fire at the age of fourteen; his father had gone repeatedly and, for the most part, permanently bankrupt; his mother had succumbed to the devastation of Huntington's disease and died in the Oklahoma state mental asylum—and still, he wrote, "I feel like in those hills I still belong," depicting himself "riding [his] pony through the draw, / While the oak and blackjack trees / Kiss the playful prairie breeze."[7]

The arcadian rural imagery notwithstanding, one crucial line stands out in "Oklahoma Hills": "While the black oil rolls and flows . . ." Guthrie's hometown of Okemah became a boomtown with the discovery of oil there in 1920, when he was eight years old. The experience of growing up in an oil boomtown was highly formative, as it introduced, and to some extent normalized, the condition of transience that would color much of his life, just as it colored much of American life throughout the Depression. Even before witnessing the worst of the dust storms, Guthrie learned to accept the wildly protean nature of his early surroundings, both in Okemah and, afterward, in Pampa, as he wrote in his autobiographical novel, *Bound for Glory* (1943):

> Oil boom towns come that way and they go that way. Houses aren't built to last very long, because the big majority of the working folks will walk into town, work like a horse for a while, put the oil wells in, drill the holes down fifteen thousand feet, bring in the black gushers, case off the hot flow, cap the high pressure, put valves on them, get the oil to flowing steady and easy into the rich people's tanks, and then the field, a big thick forest of drilling rigs, just sets there pumping oil all over the world to run limousines, factories, war machines, and fast trains. There's not much work left to do in the oil fields once the boys have developed it by hard work and hot sweat, and so they move along down the road, as broke, as down and out, as tough, as hard hitting, as hard working, as the day they come to town.[8]

Elsewhere, Guthrie captured the sudden nervous energy of his birthplace upon its transformation by the discovery of oil. Okemah, he wrote, quickly became "one of the singinest, square dancingest, drinkingest, yellingest, preachingest, walkingest, talkingest, laughingest, cryingest, shootingest, fist fightingest, bleedingest, gamblingest, gun, club, and razor carryingest of our ranch and farm towns, because it blossomed out into one of our first Oil Boom Towns." Very soon, the formerly bucolic town was swamped by "the Lawyer Man, Doctor Man, Merchant Man, Royalty Man, Lease Man, Tong Bucker Man, Pipe Liner Man, Greasy Gloves Man, Big Wrench Man, the Cowboy and the Cowman, the Spirit and the Hoodoo Man, the ladies for all of these, the girls, and the Mistresses for the Pool Stick and Domino Sharker, the Red Light Pimper and Sidewalk Barker."[9]

Other aspects of Oklahoma history certainly resonated in Guthrie's early life, some that might prove surprising to later generations who know of Oklahoma as one of the most conservative states in the United States. At the time of Guthrie's birth in 1912 Oklahoma was a hotbed of agrarian radicalism that melded anticapitalism, labor agitation, and a particular brand of Christian socialism into the powerful political movement that saw Eugene Debs's American Socialist Party gain its greatest electoral successes of anywhere in the country. Local socialist newspapers such as the *Sledge Hammer,* the *New Century,* and the *Sword of Truth* carried the exhortations of Marxist preachers like Okemah's own E. F. McClanahan, calling for "a righteous government"—a "socialist movement" and "just society" in which workers could "organize and cooperate industrially."[10] Even as late as 1917, when Guthrie was five years old, there was enough radical spirit left in the state to spark what became known as the "Green Corn Rebellion," when hundreds of Oklahoma's tenant farmers attempted a march on Washington to challenge the president, Woodrow Wilson, and the Conscription Act. The Industrial Workers of the World—"the Wobblies"—maintained a tenacious foothold in the Oklahoma oil fields until they were driven underground by the great "Red Scares" of 1919–20.

All this agitation made its mark on Woody Guthrie's own household. His father, Charlie, was a political firebrand—reactionary, for the most part, supporting the Ku Klux Klan not so much for their racism (which he also shared) as their hatred of socialism. He fired off a series of diatribes in the local press, under such alarmist titles as "Socialism the Enemy of Christian Religion," "Socialism Urges Negro Equality," and "Free Love the Fixed Aim of Socialism."[11] Woody later recalled: "Papa was a hard nut on the topic of capitalism, Socialism, public ownership, and free enterprise, and loved the chance to quote pages and paragraphs out of the thousand-dollar leatherback law library he had owned ten or twelve years ago, back in Okemah. Papa had tried to teach me to hate and despise, and to insult and fight the Socialists in any spot I got the time and chance."[12]

Inevitably, as is so often the case, the parental pressure had opposite its intended effect:

> At the age of about four or five years old, a long time before I went to
> school, I remember my dad used to teach me little political speeches
> and rhymes. And I'd climb up in a hay wagon around all the political
> meetings and rallies they had on the streets, and I'd make my little
> speeches. And it might be that I've turned out now where I don't
> believe the speeches anymore, and I make speeches just the opposite.[13]

Guthrie was thus clearly primed for an acute political and social awakening when, in April 1935, the worst dust storms of the century ravaged the American Midwest. By then he had moved to Pampa to work for his father, who was running a ramshackle boardinghouse, following the dissolution of the family unit in Okemah. Pampa, Guthrie recalled, was "mainly a scattering of little old shacks. They was built to last a few months; built out of old rotten boards, flattened oil barrels, buckets, sheet iron, crates of all kinds, and gunny sacks. Some were lucky enough to have a floor, others just the dusty old dirt."[14] Already Pampa was far down on its luck, with the end of the oil boom and the steady depopulation of the town: "Oil field drying out, the boom chasers trickled out down the road in long strings of high-loaded cars."[15] It wasn't only the oil workers who were suffering. Nineteen thirty-five, recalled one Pampa resident, was "a year of disaster for the farmer—drought, dust, then a plague of grasshoppers."[16] And if the "hoppers" weren't enough, there were the jackrabbits, swarms of them emerging in thousands from no one knew where, devouring what few plants and crops remained. "They ate everything green there was," one woman remembered. "The farmers had killed off the coyotes and that upset the natural order of things, and the rabbits just exploded and they would eat anything green they found."[17]

If there was indeed a biblical aura to the plagues visited upon the Midwest in the "dirty thirties," as they came to be called, it was not lost upon many of the "Dust Bowlers" themselves. It was almost as though an angry God were visiting divine retribution upon a wicked people. After one of the worst of the "black blizzards," the monstrous dust storms that would blot out the sun at midday, an Oklahoma paper, the *Boise City News,* carried as its headline a quotation from the book of Ezekiel: "Behold, I have smitten my hand at thy dishonest gain which thou has made, and at thy blood which has been in the midst of thee."[18] One Oklahoman, Caroline Henderson, wrote to the secretary of agriculture, Henry A. Wallace, of "a revival preacher" in her parish who had proclaimed the drought and the dust "a direct punishment for our sins": "Some would-be prophets are sure that the days of grace and mercy and rain for this great prairie land are forever past; that the future promises only hopeless and permanent desert conditions."[19] Guthrie himself recalled for Lomax his witnessing of the great dust storm of April 14, 1935, in Pampa:

> And so we watched the dust storm come up like the Red Sea closin' in on the Israel children. . . . So we got to talking, you know. And a lot of people in the crowd that was religious minded, and they was up pretty well on the Scriptures, and they said, "Well, boys, girls, friends and relatives, this is the end. . . . This is the end of the world. People ain't been livin' right. Human race ain't been treatin' each other right. And robbin' each other in different ways with fountain pens, guns, and havin' wars and killin' each other and shootin' around. So, the feller that made this world, he's worked up this dust storm. . . ." Time had come when the river was there to cross.[20]

In fact, the retribution (if so it was) had come not for any of these sins, but rather for those of the "sod busters" who had stripped the prairie of its natural protective grasses, mobilized an army of Ford tractors and combine harvesters, planted the harshest of cash crops—wheat and cotton, mostly— and brought about what Dust Bowl historian Donald Worster has called "the most severe environmental catastrophe in the entire history of the white man on this continent. In no other instance was there greater or more sustained damage to the American land, and there have been few times when so much tragedy was visited on its inhabitants."[21]

Of course, it would be an oversimplification to blame the dust and the drought solely for the great demographic upheaval that was to mark the latter half of the thirties. There was the fact that the majority of the Dust Bowl region's farmers were tenants, already caught in a spiral of debt brought about by previous years of poor harvests and virtual enslavement to the crop-lien system that had kept them permanently in the red. Behind this lay the greater tragedy of the Depression itself, which had hit workers and families far beyond the agricultural sector. There were merchants, grocers, teachers, salesmen, engineers, even bankers thrown onto the bread lines.[22] But for Guthrie, it was the confluence of the oil bust and the dust that appears to have sparked his creative activism: "And there on the Texas plains right in the dead center of the dust bowl, with the oil boom over and the wheat blowed out and the hard-working people just stumbling about, bothered with mortgages, debts, bills, sickness, worries of every blowing kind, I seen there was plenty to make up songs about."[23]

And so he tried his hand at transforming epic disaster into narrative song, drawing from a bag of rhetorical tricks to capture the range of emotions that could convey the immensity, the otherworldly nature of the Dust Bowl experience. There was, most immediately, the terror that he inscribed into one of the first of his *Dust Bowl Ballads*—"The Great Dust Storm," alternately titled "Dust Storm Disaster":

> On the 14th day of April of 1935,
> There struck the worst of dust storms that ever filled the sky.
> You could see that dust storm comin', the cloud looked
> deathlike black,
> And through our mighty nation, it left a dreadful track.

While the trope of "doom" is repeated consistently enough throughout this song, which indeed manages to convey the terror of the townsfolk "huddled into their oil boom shacks," the crying children battered by the winds and the sand, and the desolation left in the wake of the storm—the wheat fields, houses, barns, and fences left buried beneath "a rippling ocean of dust"[24]— Guthrie seized early on the power of wry humor to reflect not only a social or political commentary but also the resilient spirit of the Dust Bowlers themselves.

Perhaps too little critical attention has been paid to the relationship between humor and such disasters as the Dust Bowl—an odd lapse, given the ubiquity of commentary, from Sigmund Freud to such comedic writers as Kurt Vonnegut, who has defined "black humor" or "gallows humor" as

Son of farmer in Dust Bowl, Cimarron County, Oklahoma.
Arthur Rothstein, photographer. Farm Security Administration, Office
of War Information Photograph Collection, Library of Congress Prints and
Photographs Division, Washington, DC (LC-DIG-fsa-8b38282).

"laughing in the middle of political helplessness . . . It's humor about weak, intelligent people in hopeless situations."[25] It is true, very few personal recollections of the Dust Bowl are humorous, however much they, too, are the responses of powerless, helpless people caught up in a matrix of events far larger and more complex than they are able to comprehend. Worster succeeds in capturing—in a brief description—the immensity of this matrix and, implicitly, the helplessness of individuals or families caught up in it:

That the thirties were a time of great crisis in American, indeed, in world, capitalism has long been an obvious fact. The Dust Bowl, I believe, was part of that same crisis. It came about because the expansionary energy of the United States had finally encountered a volatile, marginal land, destroying the delicate ecological balance that had evolved there. We speak of farmers and plows on the plains and the damage they did, but the language is inadequate. What brought them to the region was a social system, a set of values, an economic order.[26]

For Worster, the one word that sums up this immense jumble of elements is "capitalism." For Steinbeck, memorably, it is "the monster," the system linking midwestern farmers to local banks, to distant Wall Street offices, and ultimately to the failing economy itself. In one of the early chapters of *The Grapes of Wrath,* a landowner's agent comes to inform a nameless tenant farmer that he is about to be evicted:

> The tenant system won't work any more. One man on a tractor can take the place of twelve or fourteen families. Pay him a wage and take all the crop. We have to do it. We don't like to do it. But the monster's sick. Something's happened to the monster.
>
> But you'll kill the land with cotton.
>
> We know. We've got to take cotton quick before the land dies. Then we'll sell the land. Lots of families in the East would like to own a piece of land.
>
> The tenant men looked up alarmed. But what'll happen to us? How'll we eat?
>
> You'll have to get off the land. The plows'll go through the dooryard.[27]

If there *is* any humor here, it is in the irony of a landowner's agent using such unrealistic terms of reference to back up his eviction notice. But dominating the passage—and the chapter at large—are the overtones of relentless menace on the part of the system, anxiety and helplessness on the part of the farmers: there is nothing at all to laugh at. In similar fashion, there is nothing to laugh at in one Dust Bowler's recollection, which echoes the terror inscribed into Guthrie's "Dust Storm Disaster":

> There's nowhere you can run. . . . You can try to get out of it, but it's as if it follows you, follows you, follows you. You can't escape it. It was almost surreal, the dust. You think about a flood or a hurricane, a tornado; you hear about those things. But this dust was something that at least in our country we had never encountered before. And I think it carried with it a feeling of, I don't know the word exactly, of almost being . . . evil.[28]

By contrast, the best known of Guthrie's *Dust Bowl Ballads,* "So Long, It's Been Good to Know Yuh," reaches for another response to the black blizzard that had "dusted us over and dusted us under": a comedic swipe at the grasping preacher nakedly capitalizing on the religious terror of his flock, offering them, in one version, "a cut price on salvation and sin"—that is, until the blowing dust makes the text of his hellfire sermon unreadable and he gives up, folds "his specs," takes up "a collection," and hits the road with a wink and a parting benediction: "So long, it's been good to know yuh."[29] This is just one example of what Edward Comentale calls Guthrie's "jocular fever," his "rambling funny streak," self-conscious and political, a "comedy of dust" that "spreads across the land, dissolving, leveling all in its path, washing away the romantic abstractions of modern life, the egotism and entrepreneurial violence of the market, forcing, enabling, inspiring its victims to pursue new paths across the terrain, to mark it in more useful, more satisfying ways."[30]

Comentale is quite right in deeming Guthrie's comedic expression a means of "liberation."[31] This, too, connects the comedy of Guthrie's *Dust Bowl Ballads* with those liberating aspects of gallows humor described by Vonnegut. Laughter is, among other things, an expression of empowerment to otherwise powerless people, as Alexander Herzen argued almost 160 years ago: "House serfs have no right to smile in the presence of their masters. Only equals can laugh amongst themselves."[32] In Guthrie's case, the laughter of his Dust Bowl migrants is one means of presenting them as equal to the calamitous magnitude of the "Dust Bowl Disaster." The cultural historian Michael Denning has observed, "Guthrie refuses the tragic tone that characterizes many of the accounts of the Dust Bowl. His one attempt to turn the storm into a tragic narrative, the unsuccessful ballad 'The Great Dust Storm' ['Dust Storm Disaster'], has the diction of Victorian melodrama. . . . Guthrie's successful ballads of the Dust Bowl are instances of his gallows humor, laughing in the face of the dust."[33]

One of the most powerful of Guthrie's rhetorical strategies was to exploit the laconic humor of the talking blues genre, for which he became well known. Guthrie's celebrated "Talking Dust Bowl Blues" depicts the westward journey of a migrant family in their "Ford machine," beset by such obstacles as a notorious "hairpin turn" on a mountain road:

Man alive, I'm a-tellin' you, the fiddles and guitars really
flew.
That Ford took off like a flying squirrel an' it flew halfway
around the world.
Scattered wives and childrens all over the side of that
mountain.

And all that awaits these hopeful migrants in California is "a tater stew" so
thin that "you could read a magazine right through it"—so thin that, perhaps, "Some of these here politicians coulda seen through it."[34]

Martin Butler, for one, has noted Guthrie's recourse to the talking
blues form as a potent indication of his satirical intent, given its origins as
a black musical discourse often delivered at the expense of white suprem-
acist assumptions: "Guthrie used a musical form which was ideologically
charged and, due to its satirical potential, particularly apt to provide its
migrant listeners with a feeling of collective identity."[35] Country music
historian Tony Russell notes the prevailing uncertainty over Guthrie's
initial exposure to the talking blues, however much his ultimate success
with the genre is recognized. Guthrie would certainly have known of the
enormously popular Otto Gray and His Oklahoma Cowboys, generally
accepted as the prototype for the cowboy bands that Guthrie and his cro-
nies emulated in Pampa, and a band that included the talking blues in its
repertoire.[36] Still, as Russell points out, Guthrie's inspiration may well have
come from elsewhere: "Possibly he was acquainted with [Chris] Bouchillon's records. Maybe he tuned into the Grand Ole Opry one day and heard
Robert Lunn, 'The Talking Blues Man,' another exponent of comic-story-
telling-with-guitar in the Bouchillon mode." In the end, it was the final
result that mattered: "Whatever his inspiration, he gave the talking blues
a characteristic twist, exchanging the joke-book cracks for political satire,
leaving a signpost to be followed by his young admirer from the Minnesota
Iron Range"—namely, Bob Dylan.[37]

If Guthrie's talking blues are comedic powerhouses, the same can surely
be said of his singing blues. His "Dust Pneumonia Blues" takes on a whole
host of satirical targets, whether, in one version, the popularity of Jimmie

Rodgers's yodeling blues style—"Now there ought to be some yodelin' in this song / But I can't yodel for the rattlin' in my lung"[38]—or, in another version, do-nothing politicians ("Now when I die just lay me on the ground / Let sixteen senators blow my dust around"), venal financial dealers ("And when I die, if the banker wants to see me / I'll be rollin' and a-blowin' in every grain of dust you see"), or the entire exploiting class ("Yes, it's dust pneumonie that laid me in my grave / But I'd ruther be there than to be a rich man's slave").[39] In his straightforwardly titled "Dust Bowl Blues," it is malicious fate itself, both meteorological and environmental, that is mocked through the simple resilience of the Dust Bowl survivors in a comedic echo of Albert Camus's existential dictum, "There is no fate that cannot be surmounted by scorn."[40] Thus, the stoic, wry recollection in apparent tranquility:

> I had a gal, and she was young and sweet,
> But a dust storm buried her sixteen hundred feet.
> [.......................................]
> She was a good gal, long, tall and stout,
> I had to get a steam shovel just to dig my darlin' out.[41]

Most importantly, behind the absurd scenario is the promise of continuance, of endurance—in Comentale's words, a method that is "boundless in its hopefulness."[42] Thus, as the singer of the "Dust Bowl Blues" concludes, "I just blowed in, an' I'll soon blow out again."[43]

In the noncomedic register—and not all the *Dust Bowl Ballads* are comic—where the laughter is gone, the resilience still remains. The most defiant of the ballads, "Dust Cain't Kill Me," makes this clear:

> That old dust storm killed my baby,
> But it cain't kill me, Lord,
> And it cain't kill me.

Nor can the tractor knocking down the homestead, the landlord evicting the family, the pawn shop gobbling up the household possessions, or the highway capturing the weary migrants—all of them "cain't kill me."[44] As the next chapter shows, the witnessing of migration and homelessness prompted more from Guthrie than satirical expression or simple assertions of resilience. Rhetorically at least, the road, as well as the migrant camps, the Hoovervilles, the club-wielding deputies, and the vigilantes, brought out the outlaw in Guthrie, as he groped toward a vocalization of proletarian resistance and the fashioning of a musical activism that would lay the groundwork for generations of protest singers on both sides of the Atlantic.

2

I AIN'T GOT NO HOME

"They didn't know what to do," Guthrie told Lomax when asked about the evicted farmers and other unemployed workers of the Dust Bowl region in the wake of the black blizzards:

> They didn't know just exactly what to do. Couldn't pay their debts—
> they owed the bankers thirty-five hundred, four thousand dollars on
> a combine harvester, eleven hundred dollars on a tractor. They owed
> 'em a year's fuel bill—that's always amounted to several hundred
> dollars. They owed the grocery bill for a year. They owed all kinds of
> bills—seed bills, and everything else. When they couldn't pay 'em,
> well, naturally they come down with the mortgage and took their
> land. These people didn't have but one thing to do, and that was to
> get out in the middle of the road.[1]

Thus began what historians have often termed the "Okie exodus," the mass migration westward of up to four hundred thousand people,[2] sparking not only a sociological and political but also a cultural phenomenon. The huge textual output spawned by the Dust Bowl migration is, in Michael Denning's words, one of the most powerful examples of "depression-era populism, embodying the 'documentary impulse' of representing 'the people.'"[3] William Stott's groundbreaking study *Documentary Expression and Thirties America* covers the momentous outpouring that characterized this "impulse" to represent the migrant crisis, from the text-and-photo productions of Erskine Caldwell and Margaret Bourke-White (*You Have Seen Their*

Faces, 1937), Dorothea Lange and Paul Taylor (*An American Exodus,* 1939), and James Agee and Walker Evans (*Let Us Now Praise Famous Men,* 1941), to the documentary films of Pare Lorentz (*The Plow That Broke the Plains,* 1936; *The River,* 1938) and the "Living Newspaper" stagings of the Federal Theatre Project (1936–1939).[4] Curiously, Guthrie is relegated to a brief footnote in Stott's study, although, as we shall see, the "documentary impulse" surely fires both his songwriting and his prose.

Historians after Stott have also begun to examine the more manipulative aspects of documentary expression that might compromise its claim to transparent veracity, whether they be the deliberate poses and repeated "takes" demanded of their subjects by photographers like Lange and Arthur Rothstein, or the studiously dramatized elements of Lorentz's films. Guthrie, too, should be viewed (or heard) with some caution; as his later producer Moses Asch observed, "If you listen to those Library of Congress recordings, you can hear all the put-on he wanted to give Alan Lomax. This is the actor acting out the role of the folksinger from Oklahoma."[5] On the recordings, Lomax himself contributes to the stretching of Guthrie's authenticity through such claims as, "He's sung his way through every bar and saloon between Oklahoma and California."[6] One of Guthrie's later companions, fellow Oklahoman Gordon Friesen, recalled accompanying him to a longshoremen's bar in New York: "He tried to play and sing for them, but they told us to get the hell out of there. This experience led me to doubt the Guthrie legend that he had played his guitar and sung in bars all over the United States, with the working-class people crowding around him and soaking in his every word along with their boilermakers."[7]

Likewise, given its many elisions, if not outright fabrications, Guthrie's *Bound for Glory* should be approached less as a straightforward autobiography and more as the "autobiographical novel" that most critics have described. With such caution in mind, we can perhaps view much of Guthrie's first-person writing, as well as the assertions of such image-makers as Lomax, in the light of Jeff Allred's description of documentary texts as "plausible fictions of the real."[8] Consider the autobiographical essay that Guthrie wrote to accompany the debut release of *Dust Bowl Ballads,* "Woody, 'The Dustiest of the Dust Bowlers' (The Tale of His Travels) (The Making of His Songs)." Of the eleven songs offered on the first pressing, Guthrie writes,

"Along the highway near Bakersfield, California. Dust Bowl refugees."
Dorothea Lange, photographer. Farm Security Administration, Office of
War Information Photograph Collection, Library of Congress Prints and
Photographs Division, Washington, DC (LC-USF34-000963-E).

They are "Oakie" songs, "Dust Bowl" songs, "Migratious" songs,
about my folks and my relatives, about a jillion of 'em, that got hit by
the drouth, the dust, the wind, the banker and the landlord and the
police, all at the same time . . . and it was these things all added up
that caused us to pack our wife and kids into our little rattletrap jallopies, and light out down the Highway—in every direction, mostly
west to California.[9]

Readers will notice the first-person inclusion—"our wife," "our kids," "our
little rattletrap jallopies." In fact, Guthrie traveled to California on his own,
through a mixture of hitchhiking, walking, and freight-hopping; his wife

and children followed him afterward. Guthrie actually hopped few freight trains in his life, yet the image of the freight-hopping hobo has dominated much of his received iconography. As he wrote to his second wife, Marjorie, in 1945, the vista he had seen on the road to California differed strikingly from the overwhelming agricultural-proletarian imagery of *The Grapes of Wrath* and the FSA photographs, as well as the hobo imagery of many of his own songs: "There are traveling salesmen, artists, musicians, show-folks, crop chasers, gang workers, road, dam, bridge, railway, and house builders. There are lots more. And there was me there in the run with my guitar in one hand and my brushes in the other." Guthrie was not only a prolific visual artist, but his first profession—and the means by which he survived on the journey to California—was sign-painting. His description for Marjorie of his daily work paints a decidedly modest picture, quite at odds with the strenuous grandeur of his "Talking Hard Work," "Hard Travelin'," and other proletarian songs that dwell on his supposedly hard life of manual labor: "You do special price tags and banners for drug stores and markets. You do Holiday Post cards on big plate glass windows. A Turkey. Santa Clause [*sic*]. A firecracker. Ice cream dishes all fancied up. You make icicle letters and sweaty ones, wood ones, hot and dry sand and leather ones. You hit every man with a new style alphabet to suit his name, birthday, personality, business and location."[10] There was thus more than a grain of truth in his friend Friesen's joking dismissal: "Woody, what on earth are you talking about? You never harvested a grape in your life. You're an intellectual, a poet—all this singin' about jackhammers, if you ever got within five feet of a jackhammer it'd knock you on your ass."[11]

If this *is* the case, how does it square with Guthrie's famous dictum, scrawled below the manuscript for "This Land Is Your Land" and carved in stentorian letters above the entrance to the Woody Guthrie Archives in Tulsa: "ALL YOU CAN WRITE IS WHAT YOU SEE"? One possible answer might lie in the example of Walt Whitman, who, in "Song of Myself" (1855), had declared himself the bardic voice of *his* people: "I am the man. . . . I suffered. . . . I was there."[12] If Guthrie had indeed been "there," in the Whitmanesque sense, he had managed to be in some historically improbable places at some historically improbable times—such as Calumet, Michigan, witnessing the "1913 Massacre" when he was all of one year old ("I'll take you to a place called Italian Hall, / Where the miners are having their big Christmas ball"),[13] or the following year's "Ludlow Massacre" in Colorado, when he was two:

> You struck a match and in the blaze that started
> You pulled the triggers of your gatling guns,
> I made a run for the children but the fire wall stopped me.
> Thirteen children died from your guns.[14]

Similarly, Guthrie never actually lived in any of the decade's notorious "Hoovervilles," the squalid migrant camps springing up on the edges of cities and along the nation's riverbanks at the height of the Depression (named in sarcastic honor of Franklin Roosevelt's predecessor, Herbert Hoover). Guthrie had only visited them, yet he could write, in the first person,

> Feller hates like hell to live
> In Hooversville;
> Gonna get the hell out first chance I get
> From Hooversville;
> Kids needs 3 square meals a day,
> Man needs honest work an' pay;
> Woman'll die if she's got to stay
> In Hooversville.[15]

Guthrie's personal experience of the migrant camps was limited to reportage. As a budding correspondent for a progressive newspaper in Los Angeles, *The Light,* he was sent into the camps to report on their conditions. As he later told Lomax,

> I seen things out there that I wouldn't believe. If people had set and told me that there was hundreds and hundreds and hundreds and hundreds and thousands of families and people living around under railroad bridges, down along the river bottoms in their old cardboard houses, and old rusty beat-up houses that they'd made out of tow sacks and old, dirty rags and corrugated iron that they'd got out of the dumps, and old tin cans flattened out, and old orange crates that they'd been able to tear up and get boards out of, I wouldn't believe it.[16]

The key, of course, lies in that slippery phrase, "I seen things." Guthrie's greatest strength—and greatest artistic service—is indeed as a witness, but more in the bardic sense than the literal sense. Like Whitman before him, Guthrie's historically dubious self-immersion is more than a fair trade for the power of his imaginative observation.

In the accompanying essay for *Dust Bowl Ballads,* Guthrie writes,

> Only trouble was that I got lost in California, as I lost the address of the railroad bridge my relatives was stranded under.
>
> However, while going through the process of a lookin' for 'em, I looked into the lost and hungry faces of several hundred thousand Oakies, Arkies, Texies, Mexies, Chinees, Japees, Dixies, and even a lot of New Yorkies . . . and I got so interested in the art and science of Migratin' that I majored in it—in a school so big you can't even get out of it.[17]

Guthrie's choice of pedagogical terminology—majoring in a subject—is not simply ironic. He certainly embarked on a steep learning curve as soon as he hit the road for California, not only in terms of the economic and social realities that he witnessed on his journey, but also in terms of arriving at a means of describing them. His education became rhetorical as much as anything else. He already had, under his belt, a host of prerequisites—a rudimentary but serviceable guitar style that could underpin his already encyclopedic store of folk ballads, blues, country standards, hill tunes, parlor songs, and religious hymns; a driving, subtle, and nuanced harmonica style that certainly outshone his guitar playing; and—as his later singing companion Bess Lomax Hawes described it—a "hyper-literacy" acquired through years of obsessive reading in the public library of Pampa, Texas, and anywhere else he could get his hands on a book.[18]

Once again, timing was as important as geography in Guthrie's education on the road. Some of the migrants he encountered on the way and afterward, when he had settled in California, had been influenced by a host of radical agrarian and proletarian movements: aging veterans of Oklahoma's "Green Corn Rebellion," members of the Working Class Union and the Farm-Labor Union, and perhaps most importantly, those from the scourge of Oklahoma's oil industry, the Wobblies—the Industrial Workers of the World—or, at least, those who had not been arrested or deported in the Red Scares of the previous decades. The Wobblies were central to Guthrie's education for the sole fact that, of all the various labor movements thus far, theirs was the first to put song at the heart of their activism (as did the abolition movement before them). For every Salvation Army brass band stationing itself on a street corner, singing about the beauties and bounties of the afterlife, there was a Wobbly band on an opposing corner—with guitars, banjos, accordions, and harmonicas—singing about the need for change *here,* on the ground, in *this* life. Any Wobbly's most prized possession would be the "Little Red Songbook" that was their activist bible (formally titled *Songs of the Workers to Fan the Flames of Discontent*). Never out of print since its initial publication in 1909, and having gone through over a century of revisions and expansion, the IWW songbook has been a repository of musical responses from a wide variety of genres, as the labor historian Archie Green described it:

> To understand the IWW's contagious musical blend, one must hear in the mind's ear rebel unionists who knew "L'Internationale" and "La Marseillaise," as well as homespun shanties and ballads indigenous to ranch bunkhouse, hobo jungle, or mountain-mining camp. Before and during the IWW's formative years, textile workers literally sang "Hard Times in the Mill"; coal diggers and hard-rock "ten-day stiffs" shared the mournful "Only a Miner"; itinerant toilers along countless miles of railroad tracks spun out pieces such as "Big Rock Candy Mountain" in straight or bawdy form, compensatory vehicles for rootlessness.[19]

Borrowing and parody were key to the Wobbly songbook; its songwriters, including Ralph Chaplin, Laura Payne Emerson, Harry "Haywire Mac" McClintock, "T-Bone Slim" (Matti Valentinpoika Huhta), and—by far the most renowned—Joe Hill, were all aware of the power of simple, familiar tunes in the service of propaganda and political agitation. As Joe Hill wrote, a year before his 1915 execution in Utah on a highly dubious murder charge:

> A pamphlet, no matter how good, is never read more than once, but a song is learned by heart and repeated over and over, and I maintain

that if a person can put a few cold, common sense facts into a song, and dress them up in a cloak of humor to take the dryness off of them, he will succeed in reaching a great number of workers who are too unintelligent or too indifferent to read a pamphlet or an editorial on economic science.[20]

Upon his encounter with the Wobbly songbook in the late 1930s, Guthrie took Joe Hill's words to heart. Hill had made his name by appropriating songs that he knew were well known to the mass of workers, such as the old folk song "Casey Jones," about a determined railroad engineer who dies in the service of his company, racing against the clock to get to his destination on time. In Hill's reworking, he becomes a strikebreaker, "Casey Jones—The Union Scab" on the Southern Pacific (S. P.) Railroad:

> The workers on the S. P. Line to strike sent out a call;
> But Casey Jones, the engineer, he wouldn't strike at all;
> His boiler it was leaking, and its drivers on the bum,
> And his engine and its bearings, they were all out of plumb.
> Casey Jones kept his junk pile running;
> Casey Jones was working double time;
> Casey Jones got a wooden medal
> For being good and faithful on the S. P. Line.[21]

But it was Hill's rewriting of the gospel hymn "In the Sweet By and By" that made him famous on a global scale. The Salvation Army singers, in their heavenward voicings, would intone,

> There's a land that is fairer than day,
> And by faith we can see it afar;
> For the Father waits over the way
> To prepare us a dwelling place there.
> In the sweet by and by,
> We shall meet on that beautiful shore;
> In the sweet by and by,
> We shall meet on that beautiful shore.[22]

Hill's parody, "The Preacher and the Slave," which introduced the world to the phrase "pie in the sky," became the virtual anthem to the American—and international—labor movement in the first half of the twentieth century:

> Long-haired preachers come out every night,
> Try to tell you what's wrong and what's right;
> But when asked how 'bout something to eat
> They will answer with voices so sweet:
> You will eat, bye and bye,
> In that glorious land above the sky;
> Work and pray, live on hay,
> You'll get pie in the sky when you die.[23]

Guthrie's early "Migratious" songs reflect immediately the lessons of such borrowing and parody; indeed, precious few songs in his entire output contain an original tune composed by him. The vast majority of Guthrie's songs are original lyrics put to borrowed musical settings—not only folk songs and other tunes in the public domain, but also published, copyrighted songs by identifiable composers. Thus, for instance, Guthrie knew that many in his audience would be familiar with the folk song "Going down the Road Feelin' Bad" (otherwise known as "Lonesome Road Blues")—which folklorist Ralph Rinzler called "a white blues of universal appeal and uncertain origin"[24]—with its pugnacious concluding line of every verse, "And I ain't a-gonna be treated this a-way." Indeed, Guthrie was so sure of the song's popularity that he recommended it to John Ford for inclusion in the soundtrack to his film of *The Grapes of Wrath*—or so he claimed:

> When I was out in California they was a shooting 2 of the Steinbeck pictures, "Of Mice and Men," and "The Grapes of Wrath." And they packed me off down there to the studios, I forgot the name of it, and they set me down on a carpet in a directors harum there, and said, Now what we want you to do is to sing a song, just don't even think, and without thinking, just haul off and sing the very first song that hits your mind—one that if a crowd of 100 pure blood Okies was to hear it, 90 of 'em would know it.[25]

In Guthrie's own version, the song gets nailed to the particular struggles of the Dust Bowl migrants:

> They say I'm a Dust Bowl refugee,
> Yes, they say I'm a Dust Bowl refugee,
> They say I'm a Dust Bowl refugee, Lord, Lord,
> But I ain't gonna be treated this a-way.[26]

We can detect other formal influences. The Carter Family's "Thinking Tonight of My Blue Eyes" ("'Twould been better for us both had we never / In this wide and wicked world had never met")[27] finds its way into Guthrie's "Ain't Got a Cent":

> 'Twoulda been better, better,
> If we'da never, never never
> Down that old 66—never went.[28]

But perhaps the apotheosis of Guthrie's transformative magic was his reworking (surely with the angel of Joe Hill on his shoulder) of a Baptist hymn turned into a country standard by the Carter Family, "Can't Feel at Home in This World Anymore." As far as Guthrie was concerned, it was another song about "pie in the sky" in the "sweet by and by":

> This world is not my home, I'm just passing through;
> My treasures and my hopes are all beyond the blue,
> Where many, many friends and kindred have gone on before,
> And I can't feel at home in this world anymore.[29]

As Guthrie told Lomax, he had this song in mind as he "rambled around over the country and kept looking at all these people, seeing how they lived outside like coyotes, around in the trees and timber and under the bridges and along all the railroad tracks and . . . it just struck me to write this song called 'I Ain't Got No Home in the World Anymore.'"[30] In Guthrie's version, however, homelessness is not a voluntary renunciation of earthly trappings or a bid for otherworldly salvation, as in the hymn; rather, it is the consequence of both a natural and an economic calamity—indeed, even a moral one:

> My brothers and my sisters are stranded on this road,
> A hot and dusty road that a million feet have trod.
> Rich man took my home and drove me from my door,
> And I ain't got no home in this world anymore.[31]

It was the moral calamity that increasingly affected Guthrie's perceptions, his philosophy, and his artistry—and it was the road that put it into perspective for him. As he would later jot into his notebook: "I love a good man outside the law as much as I hate a bad man inside the law."[32] Thousands upon thousands had had their homes and farms repossessed *legally.* Their employment had been terminated *legally.* Their savings and their future had been stolen from them *legally.* Steinbeck, for one, was able to capture the desperation and frustration of those who had been caught in the double bind of legal theft, with the culprits on Wall Street safely insulated from the agrarian fury boiling on the plains. Early in *The Grapes of Wrath,* an evicted farmer confronts the bulldozer operator about to demolish his house:

"It's mine. I built it. You bump it down—I'll be in the window with a rifle. You even come too close and I'll pot you like a rabbit."

"It's not me. There's nothing I can do. I'll lose my job if I don't do it. And look—suppose you kill me? They'll just hang you, but long before you're hung there'll be another guy on the tractor, and he'll bump the house down. You're not killing the right guy."

"That's so," the tenant said. "Who gave you orders? I'll go after him. He's the one to kill."

"You're wrong. He got his orders from the bank. The bank told him, 'Clear those people out or it's your job.'"

"Well, there's a president of the bank. There's a board of directors. I'll fill up the magazine of the rifle and go into the bank."

The driver said, "Fellow was telling me the bank gets orders from the East. The orders were, 'Make the land show profit or we'll close you up.'"

"But where does it stop? Who can I shoot?"[33]

Guthrie himself would later set such an exchange in the ironic context of selective legality, writing famously in his column, "Woody Sez," in the *People's World* newspaper:

> I never stopped to think of it before, but you know—a policeman will just stand there an let a banker rob a farmer, or a finance man rob a workin man.
>
> But if a farmer robs a banker—you would have a hole dern army of cops out a shooting at him.
>
> Robbery is a chapter in ettiquette.[34]

Out of this realization came a remarkable series of outlaw ballads prompted not only by Guthrie's recollection of the inherited British and Irish ballads sung to him by his mother as he was growing up in Oklahoma, but also by his personal experiences with some of the most vicious "peace officers" ever to grace the pages of American history and folklore: the railroad "bull" or detective, often in the private hire of the railroad companies, and the deputized vigilante in the service of the local police authority. As Guthrie recalled,

> There are hundreds and hundreds of stories up and down the railroad lines about somebody that pushes you around, and then, in time, gets pushed around.
>
> The travelers hear more tales about the hobo that lost, than about the one that won; and it's easy to understand how a story of this kind, where the tables are turned against the bull, are told over and over again.[35]

Hence Guthrie's ballad "East Texas Red," about a railroad bull who, he said, "thought like a fascist . . . He lived like a fascist and he died like a fascist."[36] In the ballad, the vicious lawman gets his fatal comeuppance a year to the day that he had kicked over the stewpot of a trio of hungry hoboes in a train yard.[37] Throughout his life, Guthrie would dwell on the bitter irony of such protected, institutionalized lawlessness: "Lots of officers are honest and straight, we all know that, but there's just a hell of a lot of them that are ten times worse crooks and thieves than the fellers they beat up and throw in jail."[38]

Guthrie turned to a fellowship of outlaws whose exploits had been enshrined in American folksong—Belle Starr, the Dalton Gang, Pretty Boy Floyd, Jesse James—and beyond, up to and including Jesus Christ himself ("the men that wrote the bible had to lay it out in jail").[39] It was more than coincidental that Guthrie's outlaw ballads should have been "popular with migrant camp audiences," as Denning notes.[40] In part it was a reflection of the wider cultural Zeitgeist of the Depression, during which the gangster film reached the height of its popularity. As film historian Robert Sklar explains, gangsters' onscreen lives "were more than matched by the chaos in society around them. Their friends, their rivals, the police all seemed capable of greater dishonesty and disloyalty than they."[41] But in Guthrie's case, outlawry went beyond mere cultural trend: he and many of the migrants whose ordeals he chronicled had seen officially sanctioned violence visited upon them personally, whether at the hands of police and railroad detectives continually driving them down the road, or at the hands of the crop bosses' vigilantes hired to scatter picket lines, break up union meetings, burn down migrant camps suspected of harboring union activists, and assassinate these activists outright—often with the grateful thanks of the official law enforcement agencies.[42]

Folk outlaws were perfect vehicles for teasing out the hidden histories of corporate and capitalist violence. Guthrie's Frank and Jesse James did what natural justice required them to do—fight, through whatever means necessary, the "railroad bullies" and the "railroad scab" who had come to "chase them off their land" and who, in history as well as song, had thrown a bomb into the James family home, killing their eight-year-old half-brother and wounding their mother.[43] In history, the attackers were most likely Pinkerton detectives hired by railroad magnates; but playing fast and loose with the same history, Guthrie not only has them killing the James boys' mother, but also gives as their motive the terrorization of homesteaders to clear the way for "the new railroad [that] was a coming through" (rather than the true historical motive: the capture of the James Gang that had been robbing the trains).[44] Engaging with Guthrie's many "factual errors," Mark Allan Jackson argues persuasively that "the history that he reveals in his songs often depends on his own ideas of truth rather than an attempt to ferret out fact-based particulars," usefully quoting the folklorist John Greenway: "For his heroes of history [Guthrie] wrote songs of praise long on truth and short on fact."[45] Thus, there is a moral truth that at least competes with the legalistic one in Guthrie's praise for outlaws like Jesse James:

> These outlaws may be using the wrong system when they rob banks
> and hijack the rich traveler, and shoot their way out of a gamblin'
> game, and shoot down a man in a jewelry store, or blow down
> the pawn shop owner, but I think I know what's on these old boys
> minds. Something like this: "Two little children a layin' in the bed,
> both of them so hungry that they cain't lift up their head."[46]

This competition between conflicting truths also shows up in Guthrie's ode to the Oklahoma outlaw "Pretty Boy Floyd"—himself made homeless (in Guthrie's treatment, though not in historical fact) after an unequal fight against a deputy sheriff who had insulted his wife. Not only does this link him firmly with the wandering Dust Bowl migrants, themselves victimized by the law, and living, like Pretty Boy himself, in the "trees and timbers," but it also links him with the roving beggars in English and Scottish balladry: Robin Hood figures and noblemen in disguise who reward the poor families that take them in. In Guthrie's treatment, Pretty Boy Floyd leaves "a thousand-dollar bill" beneath his napkin, pays off the mortgage of "many a starving farmer," and sends a Christmas banquet for "the families on relief." At the heart of the ballad is his comparison between illegal and legal banditry: "Some will rob you with a six-gun / And some with a fountain pen."[47]

Even when Guthrie turned to Jesus Christ, drawing on the prairie Christian socialism that had fired up a host of radical Oklahoma preachers during his youth (socialism being "the true light Christ brought into this world," as one had written in the *Sword of Truth* newspaper),[48] he celebrated the holy working man, "the carpenter / That you call the Nazarene,"[49] who had been crucified by "the bankers . . . the rich landlord and the soldiers."[50] But more than a proletarian, Christ had been an outlaw, as Guthrie wrote in his notebook: "He said his self that it was mighty risky business to walk up before the police, or the judge, or the Congress, or the president, and say for the rich folks to give the poor folks' money and lands and houses and farms back to them."[51] And to hammer home the connection, he set the lyrics for "Jesus Christ" to the tune of the traditional folk ballad "Jesse James."

Guthrie was not alone in making such symbolic connections during the Depression, particularly with regard to the Dust Bowl migration. Steinbeck's martyred union organizer, Jim Casy (note the initials), is a lapsed preacher who finds his true religion outside the confines of both the church and the law. Murdered by the crop bosses' deputies for his union agitation, he reappears in Guthrie's song "Vigilante Man," where his capital crime is to declare, "Unite, all you working men!"[52] In *The Grapes of Wrath*, Casy has a disciple in the book's main protagonist, the ex-convict and homeless migrant, Tom Joad. By far the musical lynchpin in Guthrie's *Dust Bowl Ballads*—a seventeen-verse epic considered so important to the RCA Victor producers that they devoted two 78-rpm discs to it—"Tom Joad" is set to the tune of another outlaw ballad, "John Hardy" (according to Lomax, an autobiographical ballad composed by the murderer himself and sung from the scaffold just before his execution in 1894).[53] Whether or not Guthrie was more influenced by John Ford's film than by Steinbeck's novel (and it is open to debate), he captures in "Tom Joad" the essence of the putative outlaw's fight for a just society—even as he finds himself on the run from the authorities:

> Wherever little children are hungry and cry,
> Wherever people ain't free.
> Wherever men are fightin' for their rights,
> That's where I'm a-gonna be, Ma.
> That's where I'm a-gonna be.[54]

Guthrie's education in "the art and science of Migratin'" did not end after he himself had found a home in Los Angeles. He still had much more to learn about the class struggle, and in California much of that knowledge came through his contacts with those who, less fortunate than he, had yet to find themselves a home in the midst of the promised land, having made their epic journey—as Guthrie wrote—"from the Dust Bowl to the peach bowl."[55] Once again, the twin forces of time and place were to have a transformative impact on the increasingly agitated and socially aroused bard, a man who maintained that his first response to California was, "Just what in the hell has gone wrong here, anyhow?"[56] As it turned out, California offered him a mixed bag of opportunities on which to build his political and artistic awareness.

3

CALIFORNIA, CALIFORNIA

The California historian Peter La Chapelle notes that although Guthrie did not "fit the classic definition of a Dust Bowl migrant," because he had not "lost a farm to drought or soil erosion," he was nonetheless "fairly representative of the migrant stream," having come from a middle- to lower-middle-income background, "fallen into the ranks of the working poor," and—most important—sought better opportunities in California.[1] Thus, in spite of Guthrie's own caveat that he was not "in the class that John Steinbeck called 'the Okies,'" he could credibly reflect the migrants' hopes (and, equally important, their outrage over their mistreatment)—just as he could reflect the hopes of Steinbeck's fictional Joad family, standing "on a mountain" and looking "to the west":

> And it looked like the promised land.
> That bright green valley with a river running through,
> There was work for every single hand, they thought,
> There was work for every single hand.[2]

Guthrie inscribed such hopefulness into a number of his early California songs, some published, some not. Hence his "California, California," where "heaven's on earth" and "Her people are healthy / All happy and free,"[3] or "By the Valley So Green and the Ocean So Blue," where in "victory and glory" the migrants "come marching through."[4]

Yet underlying Guthrie's early output was a strong ambivalence based on the enormous waste of talent, opportunity, resources, and humanity that characterized both the law's and the market's response to the Dust Bowl migrant crisis in California. As he later recalled of his earliest impressions, "I can't tell you how pretty this country did look to me. I can't tell you how ugly the cops looked, nor how ugly the jails looked, the hobo jungles, the shacktowns up and down the rivers, how dirty the Hoovervilles looked on the rim of the city garbage dump."[5] He elaborated more fully in *Bound for Glory:*

> Sign says: "Fruit, see, but don't pick it." Another one reads: "Fruit—beat it." Another one: "Trespassers prosecuted. Keep Out. Get away from Here."
>
> Fruit is on the ground, and it looks like the trees have been just too glad to grow it, and give it to you. The tree likes to grow and you like to eat it; and there is a sign between you and the tree saying: "Beware The Mean Dog's Master."
>
> Fruit is rotting on the ground all around me. Just what in the hell has gone wrong here, anyhow? I'm not a very smart man. Maybe it ought to be this way, with the crops laying all around over the ground. Maybe they couldn't get no pickers just when they wanted them, and they just let the fruit go to the bad. There's enough here on the ground to feed every hungry kid from Maine to Florida, and from there to Seattle.[6]

Equally demoralizing was the hatred and hostility for the migrants themselves—utterly perplexing to Guthrie, since California had been suffering from an acute shortage of agricultural labor for at least a decade. As Guthrie told Lomax,

> What they needed in California was more and more people to pick their fruit, to gather in their peaches, to pick their extra-select and their select apricots and their prunes, and to gather in their grapes. And they admitted their selves—these people that was born and raised in California—that they'd needed people to do that. But at the same time they looked down, for some reason or other, on the people that come in there from other states to do that kind of work.[7]

The historian Donald Worster confirms Guthrie's claim:

The large growers were glad to see this new labor pool arrive. They had over 200 commercial crops on their farms, most of them needing hand labor for brief periods: peaches and prunes, lemons and oranges, lettuce and asparagus, cotton and flax, all to be picked or boxed or baled. Their former supply of cheap Mexican workers had been cut off in 1929 by immigration restriction. Oklahomans and Texans now came to fill the jobs the Mexicans had held.[8]

But in spite of this obvious necessity, the migrants were met with signs declaring, "No Okies Allowed in Store," and at one Bakersfield movie theater, "Negroes and Okies Upstairs." As the Texan country music singer Buck Owens recalled, "Well, I knew I wasn't from Oklahoma, but I knew who they was talking about."[9]

La Chapelle has made a particularly grim and detailed study from a host of sources of the hate campaigns directed at the Dust Bowl migrants. Sponsoring "anti-Okie petitions" were the likes of the American Legion and civic organizations such as the California Citizens' Association, the Lions Club, and the Kiwanis Club. Newspapers such as William Randolph Hearst's *Los Angeles Examiner,* the *Los Angeles Times,* and the *Bakersfield Californian* all spread alarms about the "hordes of indigents" and the "migrant hordes." Corporations from Levi Strauss and Company to Standard Oil of California depicted the migrants as pernicious agents of un-American activity (read "trade unionism"), as did the crop bosses' organization, the "fascistically inclined Associated Farmers of California." Meanwhile, in government, the California legislature passed an "anti-Okie amendment" to the state's welfare code, threatening a six-month jail term for "anyone assisting in the transport of migrants who fit a new, very loose definition of 'indigent.'"[10] Much of the antimigrant vitriol was couched in unashamedly eugenicist terms, presenting the "Okies" as both intellectually and genetically backward "white trash." Not the least slanderous was the cultural critic H. L. Mencken, who, while arguing strenuously for the mandatory sterilization of migrants, wrote, "They are simply, by God's inscrutable will, inferior men, and inferior they will remain until, by a stupendous miracle, He gives them equality among His angels."[11]

The Los Angeles Police Department had gone so far as to erect and attempt to maintain a blockade on migrants entering California from the bordering states of Arizona, Nevada, and Oregon. With no regard to either the US Constitution or the limits of their own municipal jurisdiction, the LAPD set up barricades at the major points of entry at the state's eastern and northern borders—with some, like the Oregon border, being a whole eight hundred miles away from Los Angeles.[12] Although Guthrie arrived in California after the dismantling of the so-called Bum Blockade in 1936, he was still shocked enough to commemorate it in what became one of his most popular songs, "(If You Ain't Got the) Do Re Mi"—a reference to the fact that migrants who could show a hefty sum of money to the border guard to prove they weren't "unemployed, penniless vagrant[s]" would have a better chance of making it past the barred gates of California's Eden.[13] Naturally, few of the migrants could ever satisfy such a requirement. Those who made it past the state line were often faced with "curfews against migrant workers being on the streets after posted hours,"[14] or—if they dared to attempt organizing into unions—violence at the hands of such vigilante groups as the California Cavaliers, whose declared aim was to "stamp out all un-American activity among farm labor" (again read "trade unionism").[15]

When Lomax asked Guthrie facetiously whether the migrants had been welcomed into California "with bands and banners and everything," Guthrie replied, with equal facetiousness,

> No, not with music bands. They had a little different kind of band that fitted on your leg. With about thirteen links on it . . . What I mean by that is, in most towns over the country it's a jailhouse offense to be unemployed. And in that country, they enforced that when they took a notion. . . . When you come to that country they found different ways of puttin' that vag [vagrant] law on you, and putting you either to working free in some pea patch or washing dishes or something.[16]

One of the most dreadful phenomena of the entire migration crisis in California was the proliferation of vigilante activity against migrants suspected of union organization. The journalist Carey McWilliams reported the words of the California Cavaliers: "We aren't going to stand for any more of the organizers from now on; anyone who peeps about higher wages will wish he hadn't."[17] Guthrie recalled his own close call with the vigilantes:

> For a long time I heard about the Vigilante man, but didn't never know for sure what he was. One night in Tracy, Cal., up close to Frisco, I found out. About 150 of us found out. It was cold and rainy that night. It was the month of March. A car load of them rounded us up and herded us out into a cow pasture. . . . They took me off alone and made me get out in front of the car in the headlights, and walked me down the road about 2 miles. They left me out in the rain by a big bridge.[18]

Out of this and similar experiences all across the San Joaquin Valley came Guthrie's lament "Vigilante Man," which—in a case of art following art, as we have seen—draws on Steinbeck's depictions of the vigilantes who crown their menace with the murder of Preacher Casy. But in terms of art following *life,* Guthrie drew knowledgeably on the harassment he and thousands of others had faced personally:

> I rambled 'round from town to town,
> And they herded us around like a wild herd of cattle.
> Was that the Vigilante Man?[19]

It would be quite wrong to suggest that Guthrie painted California only as an unmitigated hell. As he wrote in one laudatory song soon after his arrival, "Old L.A. looks good to me."[20] Unlike the mass of migrants, he was fortunate to land a steady job soon after his arrival, joining the broadcasting stable at KFVD radio in 1937 and cohosting what became a popular program among the sizable migrant audience, *The Woody and Lefty Lou Show.* Los Angeles had much to offer Guthrie. It was the largest city he had ever seen and presented him with enormous opportunities. In addition to cutting his teeth in serious broadcasting, he frequented museums, art galleries, and bookshops. He was also exposed to a broader variety of musical styles and genres than he would have heard had he remained on the Texas plains. Most importantly, California was the site of Guthrie's first immersion into the world of the Popular Front, the antifascist movement that, with its strong links to the Communist Party of the USA as well as the labor movement, enabled him to engage with like-minded activists across a range of cultural arenas—music, literature, the visual arts, journalism, drama, and motion pictures.

KFVD radio was managed by J. Frank Burke, a leftist who welcomed the introduction of political material into Guthrie's repertoire and who, as the editor of the Roosevelt-friendly newspaper *The Light,* gave Guthrie his first commission in journalism, which enabled him to gain firsthand experience of the migrant camps without being condemned to live in them. Through a colleague on KFVD, Ed Robbin, Guthrie was introduced to the actor Will Geer—a formidable presence in the Los Angeles socialist and labor movements—and to Al Richmond, the editor of the Communist daily the *People's World,* who took Guthrie on as a political columnist and cartoonist. These and other activist figures (including Steinbeck, to whom Guthrie was introduced by Geer in 1938) became mentors of sorts for Guthrie, inviting him to join them at rallies, on picket lines, and at social events where his songs, often written on the spot for particular causes such as an agricultural workers' strike or a benefit for Spanish Civil War veterans, proved highly popular.

But Guthrie remained concerned in particular with the plight of the Dust Bowl migrants. On the radio, he tailored his repertoire to the interests of this particular audience, initially offering them a liberal dose of their favorite musical fare—hymns, country ballads, and well-known standards such as "Maple on the Hill," "Bury Me beneath the Willow," "What Would You Give in Exchange for Your Soul," and the Carter Family's "I'm Thinking Tonight of My Blue Eyes."[21] Soon he was writing songs aimed at reflecting the bitter realities of migrant life, such as "Los Angeles New Year's Flood," a disaster ballad in the Hill Country style beloved of his homesick listeners. As he told Lomax,

> When all of these Okies got to California there was sort of a natural thing for them to drift down to all the river bottoms along all the mountain streams and all the creeks. I know that I've been in a lot of Okie camps in California where a hard-working man didn't make a dollar every two weeks, and all he depended on was maybe the fish that he could catch along some of the rivers and some of the creeks.

So along these rivers and creeks that all these Okies was camped around . . . these mountain streams and all these rivers had a habit of having a cloudburst—big rains and cloudbursts that hit upon the mountains and flood all them rivers and flood all them creeks in fifteen minutes' time, a lot of times. And wash away five or six hundred families of people and take everything that they had in the world.[22]

And so he sang as though he, too, were one of them:

> Our highways were blockaded,
> Our bridges all washed down,
> Our houses wrecked and scattered
> As the flood came a-rumblin' down.[23]

He put himself in their shoes, imagining, for instance, their demoralization:

> I been a-livin' in this old town
> For about a year, I reckon.
> Every day I look for a job—
> Huntin'—and a-pickin'—a-peckin'.

And expressing for them an awareness of social injustice:

> 'Bout everywhere you look
> The rich folks own the land—
> And it looks like they just can't find jobs
> For ten million workin' men.[24]

In his "Woody Sez" column for the *People's World,* Guthrie turned to Los Angeles' "Skid Row"—the generic name for any city's derelict area, often peopled by the homeless and the unemployed—to complete his picture of the migrants' degradation. "SKID ROW," he wrote, "is generally where you land when you first hit Los Angeles on a freight train a blowin out of the Dustbowl."[25] Increasingly, Guthrie would use the migrant crisis to make connections with broader issues and conflicts as he immersed himself deeper into the milieu of leftist politics. Thus, for instance, he attached Skid Row dereliction to the American Left's resistance to intervention in the Second World War in the immediate years before the 1941 Japanese attack on

**Sign for Woody Guthrie's performance at the Towne Forum
in Los Angeles, California, 1941.** Seema Weatherwax, photographer.
Courtesy of the Woody Guthrie Archives.

Pearl Harbor: "If you happen to have the notion in your head that there aint
no work to be done except to spend all of your money on bombs—I suggest
that you take a look at Skid Row and invest your money in making men out
of bums."[26]

Guthrie's connections between the Dust Bowl migrant crisis in California and the wider world continued as the global war approached. He was initially uncomfortable with the common journalistic practice of lumping all
the migrants together under the evocative term "Dust Bowl refugee." As he
told Lomax, "All the newspaper headlines was full of stuff about Dust Bowl
refugees," but neither he nor many of the migrants knew what that actually
meant; it was "something that we'd never been called before in our whole
lives." Why, he asked, should they alone be saddled with a term that they

hadn't chosen? After all, "There's more than one kind of a refugee. There's refugees that take refuge under railroad bridges, and there is refugees that take refuge in public office. But when we was out in California, all that the native sons and daughters called us was just Dust Bowl refugees."[27] His own song of that name betrays his—and, presumably, many migrants'—impatience with the term:

> I'm a Dust Bowl refugee,
> I'm a Dust Bowl refugee.
> And I wonder, will I always
> Be a Dust Bowl refugee?[28]

Yet it wasn't long before Guthrie learned that the term "refugee" could be a powerful rhetorical weapon, not only linking the Dust Bowl migrants with other oppressed groups on the world stage, but also signaling their potential as a resistance bloc, fighting and pushing back the forces of oppression. In a note introducing "Dust Bowl Refugee" in the songbook *Hard Hitting Songs for Hard-Hit People,* Guthrie wrote, "This is a song I made up right after my wife and kids and me got out to California. . . . We lived in a little old brown house on the back of a lot behind a family of Chinese folks. They had come to this country to get away from war torn China. We was a trying to get away from the dust and bankers."[29]

Through his West Coast activism, Guthrie found himself in the midst of other refugee groups fleeing the rise of fascism in Europe, in particular Jewish émigrés. They were soon twinned in his mind with the domestic refugee group whose musical spokesman he was becoming. La Chapelle notes,

> Indeed, influenced by ethnic and political refugees from Hitler's
> Europe and Franco's Spain, Guthrie in his songs and writings began
> to associate refugee Dust Bowlers with larger, more politically
> focused struggles with fascism such as the Spanish Civil War and
> anti-Nazi resistance. By outlining how others shared migrants' status
> as refugees and informing readers and listeners about these other
> conflicts, Guthrie worked to mobilize migrants and other audience
> listeners as supporters of the antifascist left.[30]

It is probably too extreme or dismissive to claim, as does Guthrie's biographer Ed Cray, that Guthrie was simply and "deliberately reshaping himself to the fantasies of the Communist Left." Cray does, however, illustrate an important point when he quotes Al Richmond, the *People's World* editor, on Guthrie's propensity to "put on like he was less sophisticated than he really was" while in fact being "not totally unsophisticated in terms of what might be called dogma."[31] There is considerable confusion as to whether Guthrie actually joined the Communist Party while he was in California, or indeed at any time. No documentary evidence has yet emerged to substantiate the claim: no membership cards, no party records. The issue is not helped by Guthrie's impossible claim, "The best thing that I did in 1936, though, was to sign up with the Communist Party." That year, Guthrie was still in Pampa; he had not yet arrived in California, where—in Sacramento—he first picked up a copy of the Soviet Constitution, which he claimed had set him on the road to communism.[32] And as he wrote to Lomax in 1940, "I aint a member of any earthly organization. My trouble is I really ought to go down in the morning and just join everything."[33] Thus, most commentators are content to describe him as a "fellow traveler" of the Communist Party, that is, one who shares some or most of their objectives without being an official member. As Michael Denning makes clear, the Californian political scene in which Guthrie immersed himself comprised many different groups and individuals, among them "farmworker organizers, Communist militants, left-wing government officials, photographers and filmmakers on the New Deal payrolls, [and] Hollywood actors."[34] Perhaps there was one salient fact above all others that brought Guthrie into step with the Communist Party: as Wayne Hampton notes, the communists were "the only people organizing the migrant workers in California."[35] Any friend of the migrants was a friend of Guthrie's. So historian Guy Logsdon's claim is probably the most accurate: "While in Los Angeles, Woody, like many artists during the Depression, became interested in the Communist Party. He wrote many articles for their publications, but he was too much of an uncontrollable and unpredictable individualist to fit completely into any particular party structure."[36]

Guthrie had arrived in California at a crucial time in the history of agricultural union organization there. Only four years before his arrival—in

1933—a great movement of Mexican, Chinese, Filipino, and Japanese crop workers had culminated in a rash of strikes that had swept the San Joaquin Valley, spearheaded by communist organizers for the Cannery and Agricultural Workers Industrial Union. As Denning notes, "They were the largest strikes in the history of American agriculture and the great majority succeeded in winning wage increases. Because of the remarkable successes of the strikes, the factory-farm owners together with the railroads and the canning companies organized the Associated Farmers, which used vigilante violence, deportation, and anti-picketing laws to imprison the union's leaders and crush the union."[37]

Guthrie and the majority of Dust Bowl migrants had thus arrived upon an already active battleground. It was not long before Guthrie, Will Geer, and John Steinbeck, who lent his name to the union-sponsored "Steinbeck Committee to Aid Agricultural Organization," were to be seen on the increasingly agitated picket lines. Guthrie quoted with pride a poem written by a thirteen-year-old migrant on behalf of the Congress of Industrial Organizations (CIO):

> **YOU OKIES AND ARKIES**
> You Okies and Arkies get off of the row;
> You know the C.I.O.
> Get out of your trailers if you want a raise;
> We're not fooling around many more days.
> Come out of the field, boys, and don't go back in.
> We've got you out now but about fifty men.
> I'm telling you men, times is getting hard,
> And eighty cent cotton won't buy your lard.
> Tell Mr. John Farmer that we stand in a row,
> And we're all backed up by the C.I.O.
> You eat your beefsteak and farm with machines,
> And us poor cotton pickers live on beans.[38]

Guthrie found that KFVD, with its sympathetic manager, Frank Burke, and the newspapers for which he wrote—the *People's World* and Burke's *The Light*—were useful bully pulpits from which he could broadcast his songs of Okie resistance and activism. He knew well enough to tone down any socialist and communist dogma for what was, by and large, a relatively conservative radio audience. As Gregory observes of the migrants in California, "When Okies talked of social equality, they usually meant equality for whites and often only native-stock whites. When they sorted out their pantheon of enemies, they frequently figured Communists to be more dangerous than bankers. And when faced with organizational opportunities that might yield collective benefits, they typically fell back instead on habits of individualism and family self-sufficiency."[39]

So Guthrie would cloak his dogma in down-home Americanism, such as when he followed the Communist Party line on noninterventionism in the European war that began on September 1, 1939, with the German invasion of Poland. His "Woody Sez" columns sought to present the war as a capitalist venture benefiting only the arms manufacturers and their financiers—a "rich man's war and a poor man's fight"—but the tenor of his voice came not from Moscow but rather from the comedic heart of Dust Bowl country:

> As long as the pore folks fights the rich folks wars, you'll keep a
> havin' pore folks, rich folks, and wars. It's the rich folks thet makes
> the pore folks; it's the pore folks thet makes the rich folks; an' it's
> the two of 'em thet makes wars—rich folks ram-roddin' em, an pore
> folks a fighten' 'em.
>   Do away with pore folks. Do away with rich folks. Do away with
> middle class folks. An' you automatically do away with wars.[40]

The elimination of "poor," "rich," and "middle class" is, among other things, a central tenet of the *Communist Manifesto* (in which Marx and Engels argue for the eradication of "class distinctions")[41]—but in Guthrie's hands, it becomes as American as the native soil and as old as the Scriptures:

> When there shall be no want among you, because you'll own every-
> thing in common. When the Rich will give their goods unto the
> poor. I believe in this way. I just cant believe in any other way. This
> is the Christian way and it is already on a Big part of the earth and
> it will come. To own everything in Common. That's what the bible
> says. Common means all of us. This is pure old Commonism.[42]

It is a tenet that Guthrie would repeat in various forms throughout his life—perhaps first absorbed through the Christian socialism of the Oklahoma plains, but clarified and articulated among the migrant camps and picket lines of California's San Joaquin Valley. His songs, he promised, would "echo that song of starvation till the world looks level—till the world is level—and there ain't no rich men, and there ain't no poor men, and every man on earth is at work and his family is living as human beings instead of like a nest of rats."[43] He envisaged an agricultural collectivization program—and maintained that he had discovered its manifesto, which he had actually written below the lyrics to his unpublished "Sharecropper Song," "carved in the forks of a tall sycamore A.D. 1939" and "Sung way down on the old Skid Row of Los Angeles." Surely he had in mind a *voluntary* collectivization; there is no record of his response to the forced collectivization of farms in Stalin's Soviet Union, if he indeed knew about it at all, which had condemned tens of millions of peasants to death by starvation earlier in the decade.[44] Nonetheless, he wrote, "What I want to see worse than tobacco or snuff or whiskey either one is to see all of these here families of people around here all pitch in and go to work together on some big tractor farms without no boss robbing you blind."[45]

If it was in California that Guthrie first became immersed into the communist movement, it was that very movement—or, to be precise, some uncomfortable stances within that movement—that forced him to seek new pastures elsewhere. In August 1939 the Soviets signed a nonaggression pact with Germany. The so-called Hitler-Stalin Pact had a devastating effect on the solidarity of the movement, with many communists and fellow-travelers appalled at the new alliance, and others—including Guthrie—defending it as a necessary diplomatic maneuver to maintain the safety of the world's first socialist state. Guthrie remained loyal to the American communist movement, primarily for its determined, lonely, and often dangerous activism on behalf of the migrants in the Californian fields, but it put him at loggerheads with his KFVD manager, Frank Burke, who abhorred both Stalin and the Hitler-Stalin Pact. The crisis between them came to a head in mid-September when, in alliance with Hitler, Stalin marched his armies into Poland and the Baltic states. Guthrie actually praised the Soviet invasion, painting it as a liberation and singing about it over Burke's airwaves:

I see where Hitler is a-talking peace
Since Russia met him face to face—
He just had got his war machine a-rollin',
Coasting along, and taking Poland.
Stalin stepped in, took a big strip of Poland and give
the farm lands back to the farmers.
A lot of little countries to Russia ran
To get away from this Hitler man—
If I'd been living in Poland then
I'd been glad Stalin stepped in—
Swap my rifle for a farm. . . . Trade my helmet for a sweetheart.[46]

And that was the end of Guthrie's time on KFVD: he was banished. The unions were defeated in the fruit fields, and the Popular Front collapsed under the weight of the Hitler-Stalin Pact. Guthrie drifted for a time, first back to Pampa, then to New York, then to Washington, DC, followed by a tour of the South with a new young friend named Pete Seeger, back to New York, and finally back to Los Angeles—all to the exasperation of his long-suffering wife and children. Then, in May 1941 Guthrie received an invitation to travel to the Pacific Northwest to write songs for the soundtrack of a film being made to celebrate one of the largest and most momentous of the Roosevelt administration's public works ventures: the building of the Grand Coulee Dam on the Columbia River. It would prove momentous for the country, for Guthrie himself, and for the landscape of American music.

4

PASTURES OF PLENTY

"The Pacific Northwest," Guthrie wrote, "is one of my favorite spots in this world, and I'm one walker that's stood way up and looked way down acrost aplenty of pretty sights in all their veiled and nakedest seasons." As he told it, he had so immersed himself in the region as to become at one with its geology, meteorology, flora, and fauna:

> Thumbing it. Hitching it. Walking and talking it. Chalking it. Marking it. Sighting it and hearing it. Seeing and feeling and breathing and smelling it in, sucking it down me, rubbing it in all the pores of my skin, and the winds between my eyes knocking honey in my comb. . . . I pulled my shoes on and walked out of every one of these Pacific Northwest mountain towns drawing pictures in my mind and listening to poems and songs and words faster to come and dance in my ears than I could ever get them wrote down.[1]

Naturally, Guthrie left out of this account his most frequent mode of travel throughout his month working for the Bonneville Power Administration (BPA) along the Columbia River, but one on which Elmer Buehler set the record straight. Buehler, a BPA employee, had the task of driving Guthrie from location to location in a "nice shiny 1940 black Hudson"—which, Guthrie's son Arlo confirmed, worked wonders for Guthrie's self-esteem: "This is one of those occasions that he was somebody. I think he felt kind of special. Not everybody gets a chauffeur-driven car up and down, and saying 'Take me here, show me that' or whatever." But far more importantly, the

Woody Guthrie in Oregon, c. 1941. Photographer unknown.
Courtesy of the Woody Guthrie Archives.

younger Guthrie made clear what was really at the heart of his father's pride: "He really saw himself for the first time in his life as being on the inside of a worthwhile, monumental, world-changing, nature-challenging, huge—beyond belief—thing."[2]

This "huge—beyond belief—thing" was not simply the Grand Coulee Dam itself, the massive structure that marked the largest of the New Deal's dam-building projects ("with enough concrete in it to lay a sixteen-foot-wide highway from New York City to Seattle to Los Angeles and back to New York").[3] As Leonard Ortolano and Katherine Kao Kushing wrote in an official case study on the dam, Franklin Roosevelt's "principal objective in building a dam at the Grand Coulee was to make good on campaign promises by putting unemployed people to work building the dam."[4] That alone would have been enough to bring Guthrie on board, but more than this, it was to Guthrie—as Joe Klein notes—"what socialism would be like when it came to the United States."[5] Against the fierce opposition of privately owned power companies, Roosevelt had made the publicly funded rural electrification system one of the earliest priorities of his presidency, envisaging not only a massive boost for the reputation of his Public Works Administration but also a means of ensuring lower prices for electricity than the private utility companies were likely to charge.

The BPA administrators were aware that such a massive and contentious enterprise would require an equally massive propaganda machine to win the argument for public ownership with the voters and the bond-buyers who would ultimately fund the construction. Under their chief information officer, Steven Kahn, they were to produce a feature-length film extolling the virtues of the project, its benefits to labor and agriculture, and—in the spirit of the times in the midst of the Depression and on the eve of the Second World War—its indispensability for the welfare of democracy and the "common man." Kahn contacted Alan Lomax at the Library of Congress, asking if he knew of any folksingers who might fit the bill in providing a common-touch soundtrack for the film; Lomax immediately connected him with Guthrie. As Pete Seeger recalled, "Woody got paid a regular salary, and he did what he was best at: made up song after song after song after song after song."[6] In the end, he wrote twenty-six songs for the project.

Guthrie's Columbia River anthems were unique for a number of reasons. Not only were they the first of his songs to be written on commission, but, in Wayne Hampton's words, they were "among his first to reflect [a] utopian working-class romanticism."[7] Indeed, they would be highly visible—or, more pertinently, audible—weapons in the fight for public works and labor's place in it. As Guthrie wrote to a singing colleague, Millard Lampell, "The big private owned [companies] hire 2 bit movie people to tour the country on band wagons, and under big spot lights—to sing how good it feels to be so dam[n] unhappy. . . . But if the govt. even so much as hires one poor old farmer boy to go around picking a guitar and singing about People's Power + Lights the Washington crooks yell, 'The govt. has went into the show business!'"[8] So enthusiastic was Guthrie to be part of this propaganda battle that "he allowed someone to edit his work for the first time in his life"[9]—this was Kahn, who recalled nearly six decades later:

> I wanted to make sure that every day he produced . . . like in Holly-
> wood, they require a script writer to turn out three pages a day . . .
> no matter how good or bad it is. He had to bring in three pages, and
> some of it I thought was pretty poor; we didn't even record some of
> them. He had a great tendency to throw in songs he'd written before
> and just change a few lines. I didn't mind that if they were appropri-
> ate, but I wanted something that would be usable in a film.[10]

More to the point, Kahn wanted something that "would be easy to take," both aesthetically and politically—"hard-hitting stuff but not so hard hitting that it would be didactic." (Kahn was also concerned about his new charge's capacity to fan the flames of the anticommunist paranoia increasingly infecting the government agencies: "Guthrie's songs indicated he was in the class struggle pretty deep. . . . I didn't want to film anything that would incriminate me.")[11]

Of the twenty-six songs that Guthrie wrote that month along the Colum-bia River, only eighteen were eventually recorded. Of those eighteen, only three made it into Kahn's severely truncated film, *The Columbia: America's Greatest Power Stream,* which was finally released by the BPA in 1949. (The exigencies of the Second World War meant that the initial full-length project was shelved.)[12] In the final short film, excerpts from Guthrie's songs—"Roll, Columbia, Roll," "Pastures of Plenty," and "Biggest Thing That Man Has Ever Done"—are interspersed with a dramatic orchestral score by William Lava and an equally dramatic narrative written by Kahn himself.

The film might be forgettable if it weren't for one important fact: it was originally commissioned before the war, when the United States was by no means unified in its commitment to military intervention or even material support to Britain through the lend-lease program. During the initial stages of the film's production, many in the American communist movement, including Guthrie, were firmly against any US involvement in the war, but all that changed in June 1941, when Hitler broke his nonaggression pact with Stalin and invaded Russia. By 1949, with the war won, the Grand Coulee Dam completed (1942), and the rewritten film looking back on its history, viewers could perceive the shift in the dam project's objectives—from peace-time public works development in the midst of the Depression to wartime materiel production in the wake of Pearl Harbor. The same shift is percep-tible across the body of Guthrie's Columbia River songs, even those that didn't make it into the film. He began writing them a month before Hitler's invasion of Russia; by the time he recorded them, he was fully committed to the war effort and had rewritten many of the songs to reflect that new commitment.

It is instructive to follow the film's narration and Guthrie's musical interludes as this shift of emphasis is played out. At the outset, Guthrie is heard singing of the "great and peaceful river" nestling in the Columbia gorge—"just as close to heaven as my travelin' feet have been." As he fades out and the narrator takes over, we learn of Thomas Jefferson's vision of "an empire of freedom in the far Northwest," the explorations of Lewis and Clark, and the ultimate realization of Jefferson's vision: "a colonial empire sending out its boundless resources to the far corners of the earth." Within a few sentences, the sweeping history is brought up to the 1930s—the decade of Guthrie's maturation and the onset of his political awareness and musical activism:

> With the Depression of the Thirties, the nation again looked
> hopefully to the Northwest frontier, seeking opportunity in a still
> undeveloped country. But the Northwest, too, was feeling the impact
> of a world-wide depression. More than half the industrial workers
> were in forest industries. And the world no longer called for the logs
> and lumber of the Northwest. Mills were abandoned; some never to
> reopen. So there were no jobs for incoming workers. Everywhere, the
> same story: men looking for work. Not finding it.[13]

At this point in the film, the explicit linkage to Guthrie's own background is made, establishing the reason why, of all possible songwriters, he should have been the one engaged for the soundtrack: "On the heels of the unem-ployed came the victims of the Dust Bowl, a people burned out by wind and drought." Over a series of film clips depicting the dust storms, the battered farm families, the oceans of sand burying the once-fertile prairie, and the long line of Ford Model-Ts piled high with furniture disappearing along the

Riggers at work on the Grand Coulee Dam. F. B. Pomeroy, photographer. Farm Security Administration, Office of War Information Photograph Collection, Library of Congress Prints and Photographs Division, Washington, DC (FSA/OWI COLL - J 5934).

highway, Guthrie's voice fades in, singing lines to "Pastures of Plenty" that would not appear in any subsequent recording: "Arizona, California, we'll make all your crops. / Then it's northward to Oregon to gather your hops, / Strawberries, cherries and apples the best, / In that land full of promise, the Pacific Northwest."[14]

Soon the narration focuses on the Grand Coulee Dam as a project seemingly designed as a specific remedy for the Dust Bowl crisis (although, in reality, it was much more than that): "An endless string of refugees from the Dust Bowl gazed at the arid acres and moved on. Broken wagon wheels and bleached cattle bones were warning enough. If they were to find land, they must first bring the Columbia water to the lifeless acres. And the Grand Coulee Dam was the answer." Thus did the Pacific Northwest stake its claim as an alternative Eden to California for the Dust Bowl migrants, a claim that

Guthrie was happy to articulate in his next song for the soundtrack, "Roll, Columbia, Roll" (with a verse that he had also worked into the more popular "Grand Coulee Dam"): "Uncle Sam took up the challenge in the year of Thirty-Three / For the farmers and the workers and for all humanity." Then, with a snippet of his famous bragging song, "Biggest Thing That Man Has Ever Done" (aka "The Great Historical Bum") whittled down from its original seventeen verses, Guthrie hammers home the magnitude of the BPA project: "The big Grand Coulee Dam in the State of Washington / Is just about the biggest thing that man has ever done."[15]

The film inaugurates the momentous shift from peacetime to wartime production with a brief passage that (quite expectedly for a propaganda project of this nature) elides the political and moral complexities of America's participation in the war—complexities that, as will be seen, are fundamental to the history of Guthrie's Columbia River output. After a brief musical interlude, the narrator intones,

> So the power of the Columbia truly became America's strong right arm: lifelines of liberty, taking a million horsepower out of the river canyon; twenty-five hundred miles of shining circuits; using the strength of the Columbia to build ships faster than they were ever built before. But most important of all: making the wings for America—the aluminum for one out of every three of our fighting planes. Half a billion pounds a year. Building the fortresses to keep the war from our shores.[16] To turn the tide of battle. Save the lives of our fighting men. In the barren hills below Grand Coulee the stream grew warmer, and—almost magically—the atomic bomb was born. Thus the power of the Columbia brought our boys back from the Pacific two years sooner than they had dared hope.

Reflecting Guthrie's own about-face on the war from noninterventionist to ardent supporter (just as he would volte-face on the atom bomb, initially praising it before condemning it), "Pastures of Plenty" is brought back in to confirm his pride in the work of the great dam he has championed: "Look down in the canyon and there you will see / Grand Coulee showers her blessings on me / My land I'll defend with my life if it be / 'Cause my pastures of plenty must always be free." His final musical comment, again via a brief snippet of "Pastures of Plenty," sees the American home front restored to its presumably natural order ("natural," that is, for the sexual politics of 1949) with a line that also appears in no subsequent recorded version—"It takes home-loving mothers and strong-hearted men"—and a reaffirmation of the Dust Bowl migrants' part in securing the victory: "Every state of this union us migrants has been / 'Long the edge of your cities you'll see us and then / We have come with the dust and we're gone with the wind."[17]

We know that shortly after completing the first drafts of his Columbia River songs, Guthrie learned about the Nazi invasion of Russia and said to Pete Seeger, "Well, I guess we're not going to be singing any more of them peace songs."[18] This change of position—or "flip-flop," as Guthrie happily called it[19]—informs a number of the Columbia River songs, both recorded and unrecorded, providing a deeper understanding of the watershed that marked the peacetime/wartime narrative of the BPA film. It also enables us to identify some significant instances of editorial meddling in Guthrie's songs on the part of the BPA administrators. As Bill Nowlin, the producer of Rounder Records, has noted, Guthrie's own compositional habits often make it difficult to settle on a recognized, definitive version of a song: "As a creative songwriter and singer, it's only natural that he sometimes changed the words to songs, consciously or unconsciously, at times adding to the lyrics we hear here and at other times dropping stanzas, singing different words, and the like. As he himself once declared, 'A folk singer never sings a song the same way twice.'"[20]

But the difficulty is compounded in such instances as a BPA songbook version of "Roll On, Columbia," with a verse added in 1947—not by Guthrie but by his friend Michael Loring:

> Tom Jefferson's vision would not let him rest,
> An empire he saw in the Pacific Northwest.
> Sent Lewis and Clark and they did the rest;
> Roll on, Columbia, Roll On![21]

This might be innocuous were it not for the fact that "Roll On, Columbia" was adopted as the official Washington State folk song in 1987. This "official" version, posted on the state government's website, includes this additional verse while affirming that the song is "Written by Woody Guthrie"—and only Woody Guthrie.[22] There is no mention of Loring, a well-known musician and eventually a colleague of Kahn's in the BPA Information Office (Loring was instrumental in Guthrie's securing his BPA contract).[23] It would appear that Loring wrote the above verse to musically illustrate the narrative segment about Jefferson, Lewis, and Clark written for the film by Kahn. Whether Guthrie would have approved of the imperial resonances of the verse is open to question—especially given another, brutal verse penned by Guthrie himself, which the Washington State government wisely declined to include in its posted version: "We hung every Injun with smoke in his gun, / So roll on, Columbia, roll on."[24] Moreover, there is no recorded evidence that Guthrie actually ever sang Loring's verse; it is neither in the film soundtrack nor in any restored BPA version.

In any event, in order to appreciate the overall importance of Guthrie's Columbia River output, one must delve beyond the three song snippets that were used in the film. Nora Guthrie is correct in describing the BPA commission as a heady opportunity for her father to fill a creative frame "with everything from A to Z that you can think about a river."[25] But the Columbia—and the great dams built to harness its energy—serve as jumping-off points for Guthrie to engage in speculation and commentary about a wider range of social and political issues. He was hired to sing the praises of the Grand Coulee Dam, but in the end he did much more, revealing in the process the protean and often contradictory nature of his social and political outlook.

Guthrie's Columbia River songs offer some of his most fulsome odes to the American proletariat, both agricultural and industrial. Although he was solidly middle-class and never much of a manual laborer himself, Guthrie's proletarian sympathies were compounded when he witnessed in the Pacific Northwest what appeared to be the same victimization of the Dust Bowl migrants as he had seen in the Californian fields. As he wrote to Lampell shortly after his arrival in Oregon, "Guarded freights and patrolled highways make it harder for field workers to travel. . . . Vigilantes and hired thugs have discouraged workers who travel—and fake contractors and crop racketeers have won the hate and distrust of the farming people."[26] It was a victimization that he inscribed into such Columbia River songs as "Jackhammer Blues"—"Built your rivers, dug your mines, / Been in jail a thousand times"[27]—and "Hard Travelin'," in which ninety days' jail on a vagrancy charge is the reward given by the "damned old judge" to the hard worker who has been "a-leanin' on a pressure drill" in America's mines, "cuttin' that wheat" and "stackin' that hay" in America's fields, and "a-blastin' . . . a-firin', a-pourin' red hot iron" in America's steel mills.[28] Indeed, the world's greatest hero—the "Great Historical Bum," as Guthrie calls him—is really not a "bum" at all, but the worker who has built that very world, from "the Rock of Ages . . . in the Year of One" to the "big Grand Coulee Dam in the State of Washington."[29]

Guthrie's proletarian aggrandizements—his celebrations of the same dams, canals, jackhammers, and steel mills that populate the imagery of Soviet socialist realism—might at first glance seem the work of a "Stalinist mind guerrilla" (as Wayne Hampton somewhat harshly calls him).[30] But it should be noted that, his brief utopian nod to American farm collectivization notwithstanding, most of Guthrie's Columbia River anthems are actually odes to the small family farmer, the sturdy yeoman of the Jeffersonian tradition, whose Soviet equivalent Stalin had deliberately aimed to wipe out through his murderous collectivization program. Again, Guthrie's recollection of the Dust Bowl farm evictions and desertions certainly informed his sympathies for the small farmers experiencing the same fate in the Pacific Northwest. As he wrote to Lampell,

> Crooked real estate agents have pulled all sorts of thievery deals on the farmers who hit here with a few hundred bucks—no good land— cut over lands—stumplands where the people have worked like slaves with no tractors, no machinery, and by hand, to heave out the big stumps, only to find a dead end: no water. Chemically bad land, and, result, hundreds of vacant houses in the rainy country to almost match the rotten deserted shacks in the dust bowl country.[31]

Hence Guthrie's "Oregon Trail," along which the hopeful small farmer travels in search of "good rain," fertile land, and the "crops and orchards" that will flourish through the irrigation enabled by the BPA dams.[32] Again, it is hardly a Stalinist dream that informs "Columbia's Waters," set to the tune of Jimmie Rodgers's "Muleskinner Blues":

> The money I draw from a-workin' on the Coulee Dam;
> My wife will meet me at the kitchen door stretchin' out her hand.
> She'll make a little down payment on a forty-acre tract of land.[33]

Thus, what Guthrie envisages through the promised socialism of the New Deal is a partnership between the government and the small, independent farmers who, working in concert, will revitalize a country ravaged by the Depression—if the greed of the private utility companies can be checked through the federal dam-building projects. "You can grow anything you plant," Guthrie drawls in his "Washington Talkin' Blues," "if you can get the moisture."[34] Guthrie, then, is not wholly against the market—after all, the farmer relies on it as much as the greedy capitalist. Guthrie might angrily refuse, as he did in Spokane, to play a benefit for the local Chamber of Commerce ("I wouldn't play background music for any chamber of commerce, let alone in the foreground");[35] but he also sympathizes with the farmer who himself would hope to see the market improve ("Gasoline goin' up, wheat comin' down")—and who *will* see the market improve as soon as the Columbia River dams are built:

> Water come a-splashin' through the dam, tricklin' down across the land.
> Powerhouse sings and a generator whines, and down the hill comes this big power line.
> Electricity runnin' all around, cheaper than rainwater.[36]

Guthrie was fully aware of the anticommunist hysteria that would accompany any call for a government-owned power company. He recalled the "reactionary congressmen in back of the people that owned those little private dams and power houses out there, that didn't want to see the Grand Coulee built, because it would make electricity dirt cheap and cut down on their profits." So they would cry "Communist," the most convenient smokescreen for the champions of capitalist greed: "They can always think up a million nice good excellent reasons why it is better for you to go ragged and hungry and down and out and even in the dark, as long as it makes them a profit."[37] He mocked and dismissed the anticommunist bugbear in a blithe throwaway in one version of "Talking Columbia": "'Course I don't like dictators none, myself, but then I think the whole country had oughta be run by e-lec-tricity."[38]

For Guthrie, to sing about the Columbia River dam project was to sing, ultimately, about progress itself. His BPA songs are shot through with praise for the federal dams bringing the Pacific Northwest out of the Dark Ages and into "the light of the morning."[39] Through the "power . . . turning our darkness to dawn"[40] would come a liberation bridging centuries, banishing with the flick of a switch the entire preindustrial age:

> Now I'll milk my cows and turn my stone,
> Till the big Grand Coulee comes along.
> My eyes is crossed, my back is a-cramped,
> Tryin' to read the Bible by the coal-oil lamp.[41]

The new age would be marked by "everything from fertilizer to atomic bedrooms and plastic trimmings,"[42] with the Grand Coulee's "full three million horses" (horsepower) fueling a cheap and renewable energy source "where the river meets the sky," long after the "coal mine gets dug out" and the "oil well it runs dry."[43] What a utopic vision for a country, a body politic, a labor force, and a mildly socialist economy at peace with itself!

And how it all changed on one day: June 22, 1941, when the German armies invaded the Soviet Union, demolishing the Hitler-Stalin Pact and the American communist movement's long-standing resistance to intervention in the European war. Only three months previously, Guthrie had been writing to Alan Lomax condemning "the war scare," Roosevelt's lend-lease program for Britain, and everything else "that's a leading us down this lonesome road to the war."[44] That same February he had read of Roosevelt's speech to the American Youth Congress promising aid to Finland, newly invaded by the Red Army, and he spewed out his contemptuous "Why Do You Stand There in the Rain?":

> Now the guns in Europe roar as they have so oft before,
> And the war lords play the same old game again.
> They butcher and they kill, Uncle Sammy foots the bill,
> With his own dear children standing in the rain.[45]

But Guthrie's flip-flop after June 1941 was comprehensive. He was soon celebrating the electricity that ran "the factories making airplanes for Uncle Sam"[46]—in particular, the "roaring Flying Fortress . . . Spawned upon the King Columbia by the big Grand Coulee Dam."[47] We know that some of Guthrie's Columbia River songs might have been rewritten as late as 1944 to reflect his pro-war stance (if not 1947, when he recorded a number of them for Moses Asch). Nowlin is correct in proposing that Guthrie's "references to Boeing's B-17 Flying Fortress bomber could well have been written in 1941, since the plane had been developed in the middle 1930s."[48] But if that is the case, the songs must have been written after the German invasion of Russia on June 22, for—based on Guthrie's correspondence and other writings of that crucial time—it is inconceivable that he would have expended any ink in praising the US war machine before then. Afterward, his Columbia River songs are peppered with belligerent references to the "big bombin' plane,"[49] the "big sabre jet plane,"[50] and, most explicitly, the defeat of Hitler and his "panzers" in a late recorded verse obviously grafted onto an earlier, prewar version of "Biggest Thing That Man Has Ever Done."[51]

Guthrie would ever remain proud of his Columbia River output. In 1947, with the war two years over, he proposed to Asch, his producer at Folkways, a reissue in a special album, arguing, "There is an endless spring of good material in every part of our country, jobs been done, disasters, battles, and so on, and such an album as King Columbia folksongs and ballads would cause half of these people to grab up their pencils and commence scratching around to make up some song that's been running them crazy for twenty years."[52] He was clearly aware, quite rightly, of the inspirational power of the best of these songs. It was a power not lost, still decades later, on the federal government, which, through the Conservation Service Award conferred by Secretary of the Interior Stewart Udall, praised Guthrie—who would die the following year—in particular for the Columbia River songs that "told about the power" of the dams, "the men who harnessed it," and "the struggle and the deeply held convictions of all those who love our land and fight to protect it."[53]

As the following chapter shows, Guthrie himself was one of those who fought to protect the United States—both literally and in song. That record was obviously not enough to satisfy one self-styled patriot who objected in September 1967, a month before Guthrie's death, to a second honor conferred upon him by the federal government. His letter was found in the massive file on Guthrie kept by the FBI and now housed in the Woody Guthrie Archives in Tulsa. Writing to Oregon senator Mark Hatfield, the offended constituent complained,

> As a result of Secretary Udall's naming a Bonneville Power sub-station after Woody Guthrie, a folk singer who has written for The Daily Worker and The People's World, and who is or was alleged to be or to have been a member of the Communist Party, a local controversy has arisen.
>
> I have a 1948 report of the Joint Committee of the California State Legislature on un-American activities, which states that Guthrie was a communist. A similar report comes from the American Intelligence Service, of Spokane, Washington.
>
> Local admirers of Woody Guthrie resent and deny the communist tag line unless it is approved by the F.B.I.
>
> Can you through your connections do two things:
>
> 1. Ascertain if Guthrie was a communist
> 2. If he was, can you take some action to get the name "Woody Guthrie" eliminated as a name for a Federally owned power station.
>
> Respectfully yours,
[Name blacked out][54]

This disgruntled correspondent did not say whether he himself had ever listened or marched to any of the hundreds of songs that Guthrie wrote for the war effort. But whether it was on the American soil, on the high seas, or in the ravaged cities of Europe, Guthrie indeed found much to write and sing about in the context of the Second World War—a war he ultimately championed right up to its apocalyptic conclusion.

5

SOMEWHERE AT SEA

Guthrie's biographer Joe Klein exaggerates a little when he writes that, after the Japanese attack on Pearl Harbor, "Woody went just about beserk [*sic*] . . . converting all his old songs to a war footing."[1] But Klein is not far off: the Pearl Harbor attack only finished what the German invasion of Russia had started—among other things, the conversion of the American Left into full-tilt military interventionism and support for the war effort at home: the flip-flop to which Guthrie had so cheerfully conceded. But Guthrie's wartime experience went far beyond the rewriting of old songs or the composition of new ones. He went on active service—first with the merchant marine and then with the US Army—but all throughout, it is true, music was a fundamental element of that service. As Guthrie encapsulated it in an unpublished manuscript: "I was in the Merchant Marines. Three invasions, torpedoed twice, but carried my guitar every drop of the way. I washed dishes and fed fifty gunboys, washed their dirty dishes, scrubbed their greasy messroom, and never graduated up nor down in my whole eleven months." Along with his two inseparable shipmates, Jim Longhi and Cisco Houston, Guthrie carried "a mandolin, a fiddle, and one more guitar, plus a whole armload of new strings which we lent to the troops and sailors on all of these boats. We walked all around over North Africa, the British isles, Sicily, and sung underground songs for underfed fighters. We sung with prisoners of war on both sides. . . ." Then, on VE Day, with his seaman's papers revoked by the US Office of Naval Intelligence (caught up in the great fear of communist subversion), Guthrie "got sucked into the Army."[2]

The war brought Guthrie fully into the international arena, not only literally, in terms of the places it obliged him to visit personally, but also in terms of extending the global correspondences to his domestic concerns. As we have seen, the "Dust Bowl refugees" had already become twinned in his mind with the Jewish refugees of Europe; the victimized workers in the Californian fruit fields were at one with the struggling global proletariat sinking beneath the weight of rampant capitalism; the proud and swaggering jackhammer boys and powder monkeys building the Grand Coulee Dam had their counterparts building the new industrial powerhouse of the Soviet Union (so naive, if not deluded, was Guthrie about the true nature of Stalinist slavery). Fascism, he saw, was everywhere—sometimes wearing a Nazi jackboot, sometimes wearing a California deputy's badge. In one particularly moving poem, Guthrie reflected on how each new international experience impacted upon his own perception, through listening to the voices of the world that would subsequently work to transform his own voice:

> I learned to listen this way when I washed dishes on the ships
> I had to learn how to do it when I walked ashore in Africa
> And in Scotland and in Ireland and in Britain. . . .
> And here I had to learn again
> To say this is my language and part of my voice.[3]

If the Grand Coulee Dam had been, to repeat Arlo Guthrie, "a worthwhile, monumental, world-changing, nature-challenging, huge—beyond belief—thing," then the Second World War proved to be even more so for his father. As Woody Guthrie declared in his rewritten ode to the Grand Coulee Dam, it was the defeat of Hitler and his panzer tanks that would henceforth be "the biggest thing that man has ever done."[4] Just a year after Pearl Harbor, he was sharing with his future wife, Marjorie Mazia, a utopian vision of what the current war against fascism would accomplish: this was "the war that's going to give not only Jews, but Irish, Negro, Catholic, Protestant, Italians, Mexicans, Hindus, Indians, everybody of every race and color, an equal place to work and live equal, under the sun." This noble war, which the world had been "waiting on for twenty five million years," would "settle the score once and for all, of all kinds of race-hate." Moreover, it was truly a workers' war, a proletarian crusade that would "give everybody their job doing what they can do best, time for learning, time for rest, and time for fun and singing; nobody can push a man off of a farm, and nobody can make a family live like rats in a filthy dump; nobody can toss a family of kids out onto the streets for the rent. Singers will sing! Dancers dance! Writers write! Planters will plant and reapers will reap!"[5]

This may seem like the flip-flop to end all flip-flops; but then again, it was nothing that Guthrie hadn't seen before. By the time he wrote these words, he had been singing for a little over two years with the radical folk group the Almanac Singers (which also included Pete Seeger, Lee Hays, Millard Lampell, Agnes "Sis" Cunningham, and Bess Lomax Hawes, among other changing personnel). Initially leading the musical fight against military intervention or even financial aid to Britain with antiwar albums like *Songs for John Doe*,[6] the Almanacs had been caught on the back foot, first by the Hitler-Stalin Pact and then by the German invasion of Russia. Before the invasion, the fervor of their antiwar songs had been matched only by that of their pro-union songs; but the intervening six months between the invasion and the Pearl Harbor attack saw them shifting uncomfortably closer and closer to an interventionist stance (as Hays said, these events "sure knocked hell out of our repertoire").[7]

The Almanacs' first pro-war hit, largely composed by Guthrie, was occasioned by a German U-boat attack on the USS *Reuben James* off the coast of Iceland in October 1941 with the loss of ninety-nine men.[8] In "The Sinking of the Reuben James," Guthrie and the Almanacs promised that "our mighty battleships" would soon "steam the bounding main" in revenge . . . but they drew shy of saying when or against whom.[9] They chided—again, through Guthrie's pen—Hitler-friendly isolationists like Charles A. Lindbergh and his "America First" campaign ("They say 'America First,' but they mean 'America Next'").[10] With the bombing of Pearl Harbor, the Almanacs' repertoire took a second hit, since, under the leadership of the US Communist Party, pro-union agitation on the home front was to be put on the back burner and all energies directed to the war against the Axis. This meant no more songs about the workers fighting the good fight against the bosses, although Guthrie and the Almanacs remained committed to the celebration of the American—and international—proletariat in the context of the fight against fascism. Their old repertoire was smashed, so they quickly set about building a new one. Guthrie recalled, "We made up songs against Hitler and Fascism, homemade and imported. We sang songs about our Allies and made up songs to pay honor and tribute to the story of the trade union workers around the world."[11]

On the heels of the US entry into the war, Guthrie—in line with many in the newly converted communist movement—focused his efforts on agitating for a "Second Front" to be opened up in Western Europe (as the Soviets were already battling the Nazis in the east). A whole slew of songs flowed from his pen:

> That Red Army at Stalingrad
> Making them Nazis look pretty bad
> Gonna open up that Second Front today
> We got the tanks and we got the men
> To open that road into old Berlin
> Gonna open up that Second Front today[.][12]

Guthrie's impatience with the cautious politicians and generals in Washington (an impatience naturally shared by the Soviets) was palpable. When would the United States truly commit to the "great and bloody fight" being waged by the European democracies as well as the Soviets against Hitler?

> When I think of the men and the ships going down
> While the Russians fight on across the dawn,
> There's London in ruins and Paris in chains.
> Good people, what are we waiting on?[13]

Any lingering appeals to the peace impulse—as in the old days when he had written in his "Woody Sez" column that war was "murder, studied, prepared and planned by insane minds, and followed by a bunch of thieves"[14]—had dissipated with the attack on Pearl Harbor. Now Guthrie seemed to relish the deadly and just wages that would follow the opening of the Second Front:

> Corn's in th' shock, pumpkins on th' ground,
> Circle them Nazis 'round an' 'round.
> Leaves are yellow an' th' grass is brown

Nazis layin' all over the ground.
Some trees leafy an' some trees bare,
Nazis scattered everywhere.[15]

Again and again, Guthrie drew on the imagery of dead Nazis strewn across the battlefields, as in his earliest version of "You Fascists Bound to Lose" ("Composed," he noted pointedly on the manuscript, "on Pearl Harbor Day, December 7th, 1942, exactly one year after Pearl Harbor"), where "Along that Russian border I heard the people say / We killed ten thousand Nazis in just a single day!"[16] Guthrie poured onto his pages the wrath of a nation described in a quote often (and perhaps wrongly) attributed to the regretful Japanese admiral Yamamoto after the Pearl Harbor attack: "I fear all we have done is to awaken a sleeping giant and fill him with a terrible resolve."[17] In Guthrie's hands, the "resolve" was truly "terrible":

I'll bomb their towns and bomb their cities,
Sink their ships beneath the tide.
I'll win this war, but till I do, babe,
I could not be satisfied.[18]

Guthrie's ode to the legendary Soviet sniper Lyudmilla Pavilichenko is likewise noteworthy for its gleeful abandon over the rotting corpses of the Nazis: "More than three hundred Nazis fell by your gun!"[19]

Indeed, Guthrie took great pains to co-opt women as active participants in the battle against fascism, both at home and abroad. There might not yet be a need for a Pavilichenko on the home front, but that front was nonetheless a live battlefield in Guthrie's estimation. His "Let Me Join Your Army" makes this clear:

My baby said this morning she wanted to join the army too;
I said, "If they won't let you join the army,
There's lots of other work you can do."
She said, "Boy, I can run a tractor, I can run a steel drill too."[20]

Guthrie's attention to the home front was fully in keeping with the slogan that he famously attached to his guitar—"This Machine Kills Fascists"—which was not his phrase, but rather one borrowed from the many lathes, drill presses, and other machinery turning out the war materiel from coast to coast. Women, he implied, were the main combatants on the home front battlefield; hence his wartime revision of his earliest Dust Bowl ballad, "So Long, It's Been Good to Know Yuh":

> I can do without satins and do without silk,
> I'll eat lots of green things and drink lots of milk,
> I'll give you my blood and I'll give you my tin,
> You can make rubber tires from my whiskey and gin![21]

Women played a major role in the drive for war bonds to fund the prosecution of the war; characteristically, Guthrie chose to eroticize this activity in his "War Bond Gal of Mine":

> She took a preacher down in the holler,
> Give him a war bond, got his dollar,
> I'm wild about that war bond gal of mine.
> She met a cop and give him a look,
> Put another stamp in his war bond book,
> I'm wild about that war bond gal of mine.[22]

Even a traditional cowboy ballad such as "Ranger's Command," which, as Ramblin' Jack Elliott maintained, Guthrie adapted "to encourage women to be active in the war against fascism,"[23] could suggest a parallel to the struggles in the European and Pacific theaters:

> She rose from her warm bed with a gun in each hand,
> Said, "Come all of you cowboys and fight for your land.
> Come all of you cowboys and don't ever run
> As long as there's bullets in both of your guns."[24]

By mid-1943, the demands of the war were such that formerly unlikely candidates for the draft—such as Guthrie, who had four children—were now in line for induction. Guthrie wrote to Marjorie Mazia that he would "be glad, and welcome the chance to get into the uniform," such was his hatred of fascism; his plan would be to "use my gun part of the time, a hand grenade some of the time, a guitar some of the time and a typewriter some of the time to fight with."[25] As these lines indicate, Guthrie was determined to fight the war on his own terms, however unconventionally. He decided to protect that element of choice and head off his draft notice by enlisting in the merchant marine, which he did in June 1943. His three voyages transformed him; before his nautical service, the only country he had visited outside the United States had been Mexico—just across the border, in Tijuana, where he had briefly broadcast from an unlicensed radio station in 1937. The merchant marine put him not only "somewhere at sea" (the return address he often used in his letters home) but also in war-ravaged Europe and North Africa. Indeed, as Guthrie wrote in "Seamen Three," his celebration of the camaraderie between himself, Longhi, and Houston, the war took him far "[a]cross our lands and seas."[26] Each location had something to show him, filtering into his consciousness new information and imagery that informed

US Maritime Service recruitment poster, c. 1942. Works Progress Administration Poster Collection, Library of Congress Prints and Photographs Division, Washington, DC(POS-WPA-PA .P43, no. 1).

his voluminous wartime writings—song lyrics, poetry, journals, letters, newspaper articles, essays, and fiction.

Guthrie's first voyage, on the SS *William B. Travis,* brought him through what Houston called "Torpedo Junction, also known as Coffin Corner,"[27] that part of the North Atlantic where German U-boats preyed on the "Liberty Ships" transporting munitions, supplies, and soldiers for the D-Day landings—the opening up of the Second Front that Guthrie so desired. This voyage provided the occasion for the composition of one of Guthrie's most celebrated talking blues, "Talking Sailor" (aka "Talking Merchant Marine"), later recorded both by Guthrie and by Jack Elliott.[28] The song encapsulates in six stanzas the mission, the danger, and—most significantly—Guthrie's hatred for his fascist adversaries. On the "ship loaded down with TNT," Guthrie's narrator looks into the water, "a-prayin' them fish wasn't made out of tin" and thinking, "Gonna blow them fascists all to hell. . . . Gettin' closer and closer. Look out, you fascists."[29] But the physical realities of war hit Guthrie first on this voyage, as he watched Allied tankers torpedoed and sailors being burned alive—prompting such visions as "When My Good Ship Went Down":

> I seen six ships go up in the night,
> I seen six ships go up in the night.
> I seen bright explosions and I knew this was the fight;
> I was there when our good ship went down.[30]

Guthrie's firsthand experience of war deepened after his ship docked in the harbor of Palermo and he spent three weeks in Sicily, taking "several trips on foot through the peasant villages, the mountains, valleys, foothills, and farms, the orchards, pastures, creeks and rivers around Palermo," as he wrote in an essay meant for the *Daily Worker* but not published until 1990.[31] Although he did see some territory that had escaped the ravages of war, he was witness not only to terrible poverty and scores of homeless, orphaned children but also the destroyed city of Palermo itself. Still, at this stage of his processing of wartime realities, he made a concerted effort to justify to the world, if not to himself, the destruction and loss of life. As he wrote in the same essay, "This is a picture of one bombed city. I think I saw more than just one bombed city here. I saw all cities that are bombed and shelled. I think I glimpsed Warsaw, London, Madrid, Stalingrad, Kiev, and all of the others." Nonetheless, he argued that a terrible medicine had to be administered: "The people of Sicily and the people of Italy understand that fascism cannot be dynamited from a nation with ice cream cones. No, it takes the bomb. . . . Now, it is good to see that the people of Italy and Sicily understand the terrible blasting that is necessary to dislodge and destroy the fascist disease."[32]

But as Guthrie sailed from Palermo toward Tunis in North Africa, it was his own ship that got "a terrible blasting"—care of a German acoustic mine—resulting in his repatriation back to the United States, where, after a month's interval, he signed up for his second voyage, this time on the USS *William Floyd*. This voyage took Guthrie back to North Africa—Oran and Arzew in Algeria—where he and his comrades had their first real encounters with Arabic and Islamic culture. Longhi recalled their walking through scenes of poverty and degradation that dwarfed the squalor Guthrie had witnessed in the Dust Bowl migrant camps, with even the working longshoremen pleading with the sailors for food. In the end, the "Seamen Three" organized a drive among their shipmates for soap and leftover food to distribute where they could, as well as a quirky public workshop on "The Meaning of Omar Khayyám and Its Relationship to the Working-Class Movement" (earning Guthrie the nickname "Woody ben Khayyám" among his Algerian audience).[33] Guthrie had been interested in the *Rubaiyat* of Omar Khayyám—the eleventh-century Persian poet and polymath—since the late 1930s, perceiving in its philosophical quatrains a means of approaching the worldly struggles of Depression-era America. In the late 1940s, he would even record his own versions of the *Rubaiyat*—in a harmonica-and-guitar setting with Cisco Houston—for Moses Asch.[34] A decade later, in New York's Greenwich Village, Guthrie would enjoy listening to Muslim prayers sung to him by the jazz scat singer, Ahmed Bashir (who would in turn introduce him to the American composer David Amram, even today one of Guthrie's greatest torchbearers).[35] Clearly, Guthrie's second voyage had had a profound effect in terms of opening his eyes to the cultural and spiritual world beyond the lineaments of the American Judeo-Christian tradition.

Guthrie took one last merchant marine voyage in June 1944. Off the coast of Normandy, his ship was again crippled by another acoustic mine;

Guthrie and his compatriots were towed to the south coast of England to commence their final passage home. Guthrie recalled,

> The second ship I was torpedoed on was the SS *Sea Porpoise,* just ten minutes after we had sent a few thousand GI troops into Cherbourg. Tugs took us to Southampton where I counted thirteen V Bombs the first night that flew over us and hit around London. The second night on our crippled ship, I counted twenty-one V Bombs. We went ashore and rode on a bus to London. The minute we set foot in the Waterloo Station, the sirens blew, and a V Bomb struck somewhere awful close.[36]

Out of this witnessing came Guthrie's ode to the resilient people of London, now in their fifth year of weathering the rain of Nazi fire from the skies:

> Birds of death they flew by night;
> London City, you'll rise again;
> Fiery bombs from left to right;
> London City, you'll rise again;
> Workers work and workers fight;
> London City, you'll rise again;
> When that morning fog turns bright,
> London City, you'll rise again.[37]

Guthrie's focus on the British workers' fight in the context of the global war had come after months of reading and soul searching during his long voyages on the open sea. Klein notes that "during the year he sailed with the merchant marine, he developed a coherent philosophy" amalgamating Marxism with a "spirituality" about the power of union.[38] As Guthrie wrote in one of his most rousing wartime anthems, "Better World A-Comin'," "I'm a union man in a union war. / It's a union world I'm fighting for";[39] and he repeated the same couplet in "Keep That Oil A-Rollin'," his ode to the oil field workers whose refined output he had been transporting at such great danger over the open seas ("Old Berlin to Tokyo / Tanks can't roll if the oil don't flow").[40] Yet, while such songs explicitly foreground Guthrie's loyalty to his own National Maritime Union as well as the Congress of Industrial Organizations (CIO), it is clear that during this period Guthrie was envisaging a greater force than what he called "simple porkchop unionism."[41] For him, the victory over fascism would be a victory over the forces of division, separation, class hatred, and race hatred. From the *Sea Porpoise* he wrote to Marjorie of the "One Big Union" that had been envisaged by the Wobblies, but he infused the political argument with a decidedly spiritual flavor: "Polytheism means the worship of many gods. Monotheism, the belief in only one god ... Some people believe in many things and many unions separate and distinct from one another. I simply believe in mono-unionism or in One Big Union which includes all people and all things. This is the state of the Union for which Tom Paine fought and for which Abe Lincoln lived and died."[42]

Guthrie's war was indeed—as he called it—a "union war," a global crusade fully justifying all the carnage and destruction. Implicitly, it was akin to a religious crusade, as Guthrie sang in his shipboard anthem "Union's My Religion":

> I just now heard a salty seaman
> On this deep and dangerous sea;
> Talking to some Army chaplain
> That had preached to set him free:
> "When I seen my union vision
> Then I made my quick decision;
> Yes, that union's my religion;
> That I know."[43]

And if there were any remaining doubt, Guthrie spelled it out in an unpublished essay, "Union Labor or Slave Labor": "I live union. I eat union. I think union. I see union. I walk it and I talk it. I sing it and I preach it."[44]

But Guthrie's hopes for the "Better World A-Comin" began to nosedive not long after Germany's surrender, when he donned his US Army uniform for the first time, having been barred as a suspected Communist from sailing again in his beloved merchant marine. He spent only six months in the service, training as a teletype operator and singing, as he recalled, "in the Army camps around my barracks, the PX, the beer gardens, and the rifle ranges, hills and hollers, and down in Texas, then across the Mississippi from Saint Louis, then out in Las Vegas (Lost Wages), Nevada."[45] In an earlier confident, optimistic song, he had predicted,

> Yes, I know just what I'll do when I get home.
>
> And I know just what I'll do when I get home.
>
> I'm gonna keep my fires burning,
>
> I'm gonna keep my wheels a turning,
>
> I'm gonna keep my people free when I get home.[46]

But now he saw the gathering anticommunist paranoia infecting all dimensions of American society—even in the army where, he lamented, "they all look at my red background and get afraid to transfer me."[47]

The increasing demoralization that characterized much of Guthrie's immediate postwar period had in fact to do with more than his own personal tribulations. As he was to phrase it in 1947 (with the HUAC flexing its muscles, the Cold War inaugurated through the "Truman Doctrine" promising resistance to "communist subversion" everywhere, the Republicans in control of Congress, and the trade union movement purging itself of its radical activists), "The war is so far from won that you can nearly say that we've lost outright to the fascists."[48] For Guthrie to have come to such a dismal conclusion meant that he had seen a betrayal of all the hardship and principles of the war against fascism. As he lamented to Asch in 1946, fascism—particularly in its capitalist form—had

> killed several members of my family, it gassed several and shell
> shocked several more in the last world war, and in this world war
> just past, it scattered lots more. It drove families of my relatives and
> friends by the hundreds of thousands to wander more homeless than
> dogs and to live less welcome than hogs, sheep, or cattle. This is the
> system I started out to expose by every conceivable way that I could
> think of with songs and with ballads, and even with poems, stories,
> newspaper articles, even by humor, by fun, by nonsense, ridicule and
> by any other way that I could lay hold on.[49]

In 1949 the Soviets detonated their first atomic bomb—the device which, in the hands of the United States, Guthrie had actually celebrated when it brought the world war to its end. Now, he had turned firmly against it, writing fearfully,

> My angel, my darling,
> When that atom bomb does come;
> Let me be your pillow
> While this world's on fire.[50]

We know that by the late 1940s, Guthrie was already experiencing the disorienting effects of the neurological disorder, Huntington's disease, that would claim his life in 1967. But it seems clear that, as he penned the terrifying "Post War Breakout," he was thinking of more than his own nervous system. Reality itself appeared to have broken loose from its moorings as the world raced toward nuclear Armageddon and American society seemed to be crumbling into poverty, race hatred, paranoia, and political savagery:

> I'ma post war breakout
> I'ma post war breakdown
> I'ma post war nervroe
> And a post war hero
> I'ma post war skitzoe
> I'ma post war freenyoe
> Post war newrve case.[51]

It was largely from the vantage point of New York City that Guthrie watched the postwar American Left crumble before his eyes. It can only have proved doubly disorienting for him since the political poison had infected what Guthrie had felt was the most progressive bastion of all America: New York, which he had called "the main fort and vanguard of the working class movement."[52] In order to appreciate how demoralizing the postwar descent could have been for Guthrie, it is necessary to examine what the possibilities of New York had meant for him. It is to these possibilities that we now turn.

6

NEW YORK TOWN

Guthrie first blew into New York early in 1940, at the suggestion of Will Geer, who had moved there from Los Angeles to take up a starring role in the Broadway production of *Tobacco Road*. They had worked, traveled, and agitated together for the union movement up and down the San Joaquin Valley; but with the agricultural and canning unions for the most part defeated or defanged by late 1939, there were new horizons to be explored—and new agitation to foment—on the East Coast. What Guthrie found in New York was more than a labor movement or a communist movement; he found a politically driven, bohemian subculture that electrified him, championed him, and—eventually—thrust him into the national spotlight. The New York avant-garde adopted him—as a singer, writer, visual artist, and (perhaps still unknown to many) commentator on modern dance, through which art form he would meet his second wife, Marjorie (a dancer with the Martha Graham Company), with whom he would father four of his eight children. In New York he would become immersed in his wife's Jewish culture and, in partnership with her and inspired by their children, develop a still-thriving body of children's songs.

New York, to some extent, completed what had begun in Los Angeles: the unlocking of Woody Guthrie, who remained for the rest of his life an urban bohemian and modern cosmopolitan, virtually transformed by the cultural diversity of the city. It was the genius of his hillbilly "Okie" persona that enabled him to perpetuate the myth of the hard travelin', unlettered "Dust Bowl Balladeer" for so long—even into his afterlife—and often at the expense of lesser-known aspects of his artistry that have only recently begun to emerge through scholarship, the publication of such volumes as *Woody Guthrie Artworks,*[1] and the continued appearance of previously unpublished songs put to music by contemporary musicians brought into the Woody Guthrie Archives under the patronage of Nora Guthrie.

Regardless of the artistic mode, political exhilaration is never far from the surface of Guthrie's New York output. As he commented soon after his arrival:

> I suppose old New York is about the revoltingest place in the country. You can always go out and take a look at the rest of the country, fist fights, gun fights, strikes, police and legion raids, and everything, and then when you go back to New York, you'll see it just a little bit plainer, or the same thing in just a cleaner looking glass; you'll see the working folks marching up and down the streets, having meetings, talking, preaching, and always going the rest of the country just one better.[2]

In his "Woody Sez" columns, which he continued to submit from New York to the San Francisco–based *People's World,* Guthrie perpetuated the myth of the country rube dazzled by the big city, marveling in its gigantic dimensions and the extremity of its contrasts. Even though this was partly for comedic effect, there was usually a serious political observation to be made. "There is one and only one New York," he wrote, "it's got the best of the least for the most, and the most of the best for the least, and the biggest bunch of people on earth that work like dogs for a living, and the biggest bunch that live a hole lifetime and never hit a lick of work."[3] A tourist excursion to the Empire State Building would be a lesson in contemporary economics:

> Costs you a dollar bill to go to the top. Elevators really run you down fast. We dropt 34 floors before I could call out my number. That's fast droppin'. Almost dropt as fast as wages.
>
> After we hit bottom my pants kept on a goin'. It never was this a-way back home.
>
> However there are 7,000,000 people here in New York. I would judge 6,000,000 of 'em has already lost their pants.[4]

Again, it is the country "rube" who, in spite of his malapropisms, is able to fire a critical arrow into the heart of the acquisitive society dominated by the corporate megastructures that, in their arrogance, succeed even in blotting out the "endless skyway" that he had celebrated in "This Land Is Your Land": "Talking about the sky, here in New York you have got to give the taxi company 35 cents cash to get a cab driver to chase some down for you. That's the Capitalist cistern for you, they build up so much buildins to beat you out of money with, that they finally block out the sky, and charge you 20 cts. a mile to ride a round an look at it."[5]

Economic disparity was engineered into the very fabric of the city. Perceiving this firsthand appears to have reordered Guthrie's thinking in terms of the coming socialist revolution. As Will Geer recalled, he and Guthrie had been "quite sure" that they would both see "a bloodless revolution" in their time—but, for reasons unexplained, "the revolution was going to happen in Chicago, then spread to the coasts."[6] The political and economic tensions of New York changed all that for Guthrie; it was within a year of his arrival that he declared his new city to be the "main fort and vanguard" of the American class struggle.[7] Guthrie had found his home, and—to the extent that such a volatile, restless wanderer could ever find a home—New York would remain Guthrie's for the rest of his all-too-short life.

It is significant that, very early on, Guthrie should have been magnetically drawn to the sights and images of New York's most notorious Skid Row, the Bowery, on the Lower East Side. Just as, on the West Coast, he had designated Skid Row as "where you land when you first hit Los Angeles on a freight train a blowin out of the Dustbowl," in New York he found that there was much to absorb at the outset from an acquaintance with Skid Row. Although he spent his first few weeks living in Will and Herta Geer's lavish uptown apartment on Fifth Avenue, he wandered through the Bowery time and again. It was a particularly fertile site for Guthrie to work out his conceptions of New York's social and economic contradictions—hence one of his first New York songs, composed in the Geers' apartment, "I Don't Feel at Home in the Bowery Anymore" (based, like "I Ain't Got No Home," on the Carter Family's "Can't Feel at Home in This World Anymore"):

I seen an apartment on 5th Avenue
A penthouse, and garden, and skyscraper view;
A carpet so soft, with a hard-wood floor,
I don't feel at home on the Bowery no more.[8]

In similar comparative fashion, an unpublished essay titled "Manifesto on Wage Slaves, Sleep Walking, and Jesus" foregrounds the irony of a barefoot, derelict man "all dirty and ragged in his old greasy overhalls and black dirty feet" sleeping "in the dim glow of a street lamp a half a block away that struck and reflected against the big brass plate that said the Bowery Saving Bank."[9]

Even in his less overtly didactic output, Guthrie could scarcely resist making his economic commentary—in such songs as "The New York Trains," a comic disquisition on the confusions of the urban transport system, which notes of the common taxi fare: "And down in Texas that's enough to pay six months of rent."[10] Financial exhaustion provides a through-line—in "Talkin' Subway Blues," where the "last lone nickel" is gobbled up for a subway ride;[11] or in "New York Town," where "a little hard luck" dominates and the "last old dollar" slips away, but where there is at least a prospect of renewal, of remaking, of riding "that new morning train."[12]

Again, one of Guthrie's most celebrated New York songs, "Jesus Christ"—written, he recalled, "in Hanover House, in New York's shady-streeted city"[13]—was inspired by a firsthand vision of urban dereliction. As Guthrie described it, having watched a bearded, Christ-looking figure rooting through the garbage:

I wrote this song looking out of a rooming house window in New York City in the winter of 1940. I saw how the poor folks lived, and then I saw how the rich folks lived, and the poor folks down and out and cold and hungry, and the rich ones out drinking good whiskey and celebrating and wasting handfuls of money . . . and I got to thinking about what Jesus said, and what if He was to walk into New York City and preach like He used to. They'd lock Him back in jail as sure as you're reading this. "Even as you've done it unto the least of these little ones, you have done it unto me."[14]

In Guthrie's "Jesus Christ," all challenges to the market and the elimination of poverty through socialism are blocked through a repressive network made up of "the sheriff," "the bankers and the preachers," "the cops and soldiers," and "the landlord"[15]—all these connections inspired, as Nora Guthrie recalled, by her father "looking out over a bustling Times Square from a cheap boarding house window."[16]

Three days before composing "Jesus Christ," Guthrie had made his first major New York appearance, playing at a benefit organized by Geer for the Dust Bowl migrants in California. It was here that he first met Pete Seeger, Lead Belly, and the folksong collector Alan Lomax, who was at that time in charge of the Archive of American Folksong at the Library of Congress in Washington, DC. Lomax credited this auspicious first encounter with nothing less than "the renaissance of American folk song,"[17] while Wayne Hampton, with slightly more precision, marked its foundational role in the "proletarian renaissance in American popular music."[18] Guthrie himself was both overly coy and slightly untruthful in his declaration: "I didn't even hear the world 'ballad' nor the word 'folk,' well, till I hit New York in the snow of '41" (a misremembering, as the year was 1940).[19] But he was certainly correct in citing New York as the place where the great folk music revival of the 1940s got its kick-start—and Guthrie had arrived at just the right time.

For the previous decade, the New York Popular Front had been in the vanguard of the cultural project to Americanize and otherwise make familiar certain objectives of the Communist International—most immediately, the fight against fascism, but also the proletarian struggle against capitalist exploitation—and Guthrie was at the heart of that project. When the New York–based *Daily Worker,* the US Communist Party's organ, decided to pick up Guthrie's "Woody Sez" column from the *People's World,* it was meant to show that the party could be "interested in people" as well as "policy" (as the paper's feature editor recalled).[20] The Popular Front's project of presenting communism as simply "Twentieth-Century Americanism" (to quote the CPUSA's general secretary, Earl Browder) was reflected in Mike Quin's ecstatic review of one of Guthrie's earliest New York radio broadcasts: "Sing it, Woody, sing it! Karl Marx wrote it, and Lincoln said it, and Lenin did it."[21]

Another writer flirting with communism at that time, the novelist Saul Bellow (who had been a Trotskyite before turning to conservatism),

Woody Guthrie in New York, 1943. *Bound for Glory* publicity photo. Eric Schaal, photographer. Courtesy of the Woody Guthrie Archives.

recalled the New York of 1940 as "a very Russian city": "New York dreamed of leaving North America and merging with Russia," he exaggerated.[22] This meant that many older members of the New York Left—largely Jewish émigrés from the *shtetls* of Eastern Europe—did not know what to make of the newly transplanted "Okie" in their midst; but as Guthrie's later colleague Irwin Silber observed, for the younger ones, the "New York, Northeastern Jewish kids who largely created the folk revolution"—the "first or second generation American[s]" who were still "desperately trying to get Americanized"—Guthrie represented "the heart of America" and "was of great, great, importance."[23] Serge Denisoff was not far off in highlighting the centrality of American folk music in the communist movement's project in the late 1930s and early '40s, particularly in terms of its uses in furthering the proletarian revolution: for the CPUSA, "nearly any musical piece which echoed some American tradition became proletarian."[24]

Alan Lomax was particularly well placed to further the Popular Front's musical project. Not only did he have personal connections with the Roosevelt administration and friends in other high places in Washington (which meant access to considerable federal patronage that could be redirected to such protégés as Guthrie, Seeger, and Lead Belly), but his word and his activities carried great weight in both the recording and the broadcast industries. It was thanks to Lomax and his connections with such Popular Front producers as Norman Corwin that Guthrie got his greatest East Coast broadcasting breaks. Within his first year in New York he appeared on such popular radio programs as *The Pursuit of Happiness* (CBS), *Back Where I Come From* (CBS), *We the People* (CBS), and *Cavalcade of America* (NBC)—all of which utilized his emerging image as the "People's Bard" to great effect. Guthrie also had his first and last big-money radio experience, which he would regret for ever afterwards, on CBS's *Pipe Smoking Time* program, sponsored by the Model Tobacco Company. Seduced by the considerable monetary temptations, he went so far as to rewrite his Dust Bowl ballad "So Long, It's Been Good to Know Yuh" into a lame commercial jingle for the show. Such activities soon proved anathema to him, and he resigned from CBS in a matter of weeks.

Naturally, Guthrie's most satisfying nonfamilial relationships in New York were with those who shared his political as well as his artistic objectives. Besides Lomax himself, there were those musicians whom Lomax championed as a patron, the likes of Cisco Houston, Lead Belly, Josh White, Sonny Terry, Brownie McGhee, Pete Seeger, and Lee Hays (the latter two of whom, along with Millard Lampell, would form the Almanac Singers, which included Guthrie and Lomax's sister, Bess). Although the Almanacs would last only two years as a coherent group (buffeted as they were by the dizzying changes in political stance that marked the few years on either side of the Hitler-Stalin Pact and Pearl Harbor), they were highly influential in the history of American folk music. As Lampell described it, the Almanacs represented the first "organized attempt" to "give back to the people the songs of the workers." Thus, within the proletarian activist sphere, the Almanacs were noted for introducing "a body of music that dealt with subjects other than love."[25] Like-minded radicals such as Dashiell Hammett (detective novelist), Marc Blitzstein (composer), Rockwell Kent (artist), Mike Gold (journalist), Walter Lowenfels (poet), and various Martha Graham Company dancers all frequented the series of communal dwellings known as Almanac House, where Guthrie and his fellow Almanacs effectively hosted an artistic salon of sorts. But it must be said that, outside of this relatively small bohemian sphere, the Almanacs had little immediate impact, as most New Yorkers were perplexed by—if they noticed at all—an urban musical group promoting the rural folk sounds of the American South.

It was mostly Guthrie himself who attracted the notice of cultural observers his first few years in New York. As he recalled for Alan Lomax after a performance with Cisco Houston in a New York nightclub, his growing popularity was a direct reflection of the city's increasing awareness of the calamities being played out in the broad lands west of the Hudson River:

> The big reporters from the newspapers come down and they listened to the songs about the people in the dust bowl and about the ones that are chasing up and down that big 66 highway with empty bowls and the ones that went to California trying to swap a cracked crock bowl for a sugar bowl and the police and big farmers got the whole works—and the papers here, the *Sun* and others give a pretty good write up or two about the dust bowl.[26]

(Nor was Guthrie immune to the fallout occasioned—even in New York—by his associations with the Popular Front, the Communist Party of the USA, and certainly the Almanacs themselves. As he told Lomax in the same letter, "Lots of people wrote in hollering that the reporter fell for a lot of fifth column stuff. They called me a communist and a wild man and everything you could think of but I dont care what they call me.")[27]

Such accusations notwithstanding, one of the most attractive aspects of New York for Guthrie was the sheer breadth of cultural expression and political opinion to be found there. If the city was indeed, to repeat Saul Bellow, "a very Russian city," it was also much more than that. One senses the euphoria with which Guthrie embraced the great cultural mix of New York, as in his ode to the city's diversity, "Union Air in Union Square":

Old Paunchy shoots the Trotsky line and waves his hands and
    struts
Reef Wilson sweats for the socialists and the pigeons think he's
    nuts
Herb Solomon howls to get the dough to rebuild Jerusalem
And above it all there waves the flag of your good old Uncle Sam.

I walked around and I heard the sound of voices of all sorts
The Slav, the Dutch, the heavy Swede, the Negro, longs and shorts,
The broad flat A's from the western plains, the thick ones and
    the thin,
The same old flag flew over them all—all free, but different men[.][28]

Guthrie literally married into this diverse cultural landscape when he wed Marjorie Greenblatt Mazia, the daughter of Aliza Greenblatt, one of America's most celebrated Yiddish writers. He immersed himself into the world of his wife's Jewish heritage, writing a number of songs with Jewish and Hanukkah themes and reveling in the great ethnic mix to be found in the neighborhood of his home on Coney Island's Mermaid Avenue:

Mermaid Avenue, that's the street
Where all colors of goodfolks meet;
Where the smokefish meets the pretzel,
Where the borscht sounds like the seas;
This is where hot Mexican chilli
Meets chop suey and meatballs sweet.[29]

Guthrie's euphoria was certainly bound up in the joys of starting a new family with Marjorie. Their oldest daughter, Cathy (who would die tragically in a fire at the age of four), inspired many of the children's songs for which Guthrie is still well known, including his ode to the playground that was Coney Island:

Walk like a lady,
Ride like a man.
Hop, skip and jump,
Keep warm in my hand.

>Boat on the water,
>Train on the land:
>Go Coney Island,
>Roll on the sand.[30]

Not that Guthrie was enamored of everything New York had to offer ("We looked and walked and walked and looked and everywhere we went they said, 'Two things in this world that don't exist, one is God and the other one is Apartments'").[31] Popular culture was a particular target of his. In addition to his incessant hammering of Broadway and Tin Pan Alley as purveyors of the "fake" and the "phoney," he took many potshots at the movies (although he was an inveterate film goer himself): "I noticed in New York and in Hollywood, and I stuck my head a good piece in both directions, that the sissier, the smoother, the slicker, and the higher polished that you get, and the fartherest from the truth, that the higher wages you'll draw down."[32] Not only was the average cinematic fare mendacious; it was, with its outpouring of violence and horror, positively damaging. Mocking the usual Saturday morning offerings with such made-up titles as *The Green Evil of the Grey Mansion, Corpse's Last Kiss,* and *Murder on the Tar Roof,* Guthrie suggested that New York's children would be better off if they'd been taken to the morgue instead of the movies: "They'll come out healthier."[33]

But if New York had the sickness, it also had the cure—or so Guthrie thought—in its vast fellowship of progressive and radical artists, not least its folk musicians. He signed on enthusiastically to the People's Songs initiative, the brainchild of Pete Seeger and Waldemar Hille, whose aim—in Seeger's words—was to "make a singing labor movement" through performance, mentoring in songwriting, education, and outreach.[34] With its base in New York, where People's Songsters taught classes "on the use of music for political action," and with hubs in other major cities such as Detroit and Los Angeles, People's Songs had a short but energetic life (1946–1949).[35] In particular, the organization's introduction of the "hootenanny" or "hoot" (the phrase having been brought by Guthrie from the West Coast) helped to spread political folk music throughout New York and other cities. Guthrie described—with some likely exaggeration—the exponential growth of the hootenanny's popularity: "The first People's Songs Hootenanny was thrown in the Otah home, and eight people came. The second Hoot was up in Brother's apartment on Thompson Street, and a hundred and twelve came. The third was in the Newspaper Guild Hall on East 40th Street, and three hundred sang for half a day. . . . Seventy-five people in the balcony had to stand up. Everybody else stood up because they couldn't set still."[36]

In the end, however, New York was not immune to the forces of antiradicalism and anticommunism that increasingly infected the political and cultural spheres with the onset of the Cold War. By 1947 McCarthyism was in the ascendant, with the House Un-American Activities Committee (HUAC) reaching its tentacles into all walks of life—not only the entertainment industry, the federal government, the military, and the education profession, but the labor movement as well. People's Songs was hit very hard: the increasingly conservative and frightened labor unions, as well as colleges and other venues, avoided engagement with them, and the bankrupt organization wound down finally in 1949. Some stalwarts, however, including Guthrie, Seeger, and editor Irwin Silber, continued to fight the good fight, helping to constitute a progressive booking agency, People's Artists, and launching the folk music magazine that remains today as *Sing Out!*

Guthrie managed to maintain his political energy and acuity even as his neurological system began to disintegrate with grim steadiness from about 1953 onward, as a result of the inescapably fatal Huntington's disease that he had inherited from his mother. He spent a great deal of the remaining decade wandering away from—but always returning to—New York. As his condition worsened and he spent more and more time languishing in hospitals, a younger generation of folksingers (later dubbed "Woody's Children"), with Pete Seeger at the vanguard, began actively circulating his songs and his story among college, summer camp, and folk club audiences. Guthrie's greatest anthem, "This Land Is Your Land," written in 1940 within weeks of his arrival in New York, filtered its way into the consciousness of a new generation, mostly through its publication in school songbooks. In one of his last public appearances, in 1956, Guthrie was seen in the audience of a tribute concert dedicated to him at New York's Pythian Hall—an event that Bryan Garman has called "the point of departure for Guthrie's ascent to heroic status . . . a coming-out party of sorts for the folk song movement. The country had grown weary of Senator Joe McCarthy's anticommunist crusade, and for the first time in a decade, cultural workers could celebrate their artistic and political mentor without facing the threat of being called before HUAC."[37]

Having weathered the worst of the anticommunist storm, New York had thus demonstrated for Guthrie the resilience that he had noted in his letters, essays, and lyrics, such as "Ninety Mile Wind":

> The radio says a ninety mile wind
> Will whip old New York town tonight.
> Well, I did walk and the wind did come
> And I got to see who was the toughest:
> New York town or the high blowing wind.
> And I found out New York was the roughest.
>
> This town has stood up in the face of things
> Lots worse than a ninety mile wind.
> It's not bad storms I'm afraid of today
> But the greed that our leaders walk in.[38]

New York, Guthrie maintained in the end, was where he had found his "voice"—in the streets, in the shops, in the public parks, in the delicatessens, and in the playgrounds; certainly not in the contrived and manufactured texts of popular and civic culture:

> Oh but I have not even heard this voice, these voices,
> On the stages, screens, radios, records, juke boxes,
> In magazines nor not in newspapers, seldom in courtrooms,
> And more seldom when students and policemen study the faces
> Behind the voices.[39]

New York City—"the Hudson and East river's / One lost lonesome child," where "Ten million wild notions / Are fighting . . . / To speak a little plainer / And try to agree"[40]—took Guthrie to its bosom and became his final home. The sea off Coney Island received his ashes on a windy October day in 1967. Although Guthrie had been born in the Oklahoma hills, came to his maturity in Texas, and achieved his political awakening on the road and in California, New York gave to him its wondrous expansiveness and received from him his heart.

7

BELUTHAHATCHEE

Although Guthrie spent the last twenty-seven years of his life based, for the most part, in New York City, it was inevitable that such a restless soul as he would periodically make tracks for other locations, whether it was the Pacific Northwest, Los Angeles, the high seas, Europe, or North Africa. As we have seen, each of these places provided major chapters in Guthrie's biography and had immensely fertile impact on his creativity. One of the most important and least known places influencing Guthrie as a thinker and songwriter was what Zora Neale Hurston called "a Florida Shangri-la, where all unpleasantness is forgiven or forgotten": the mythically named "Beluthahatchee," just south of Jacksonville, where Guthrie's friend and fellow antiracist Stetson Kennedy had established a sanctuary for progressive activism in the midst of the Cold War and in the heart of the Jim Crow South.[1] Guthrie, who had met Kennedy in New York in 1940, made a series of visits to Beluthahatchee between 1951 and 1953; out of this experience came more than seventy songs, a corpus that former Guthrie Archives curator Jorge Arévalo Mateus ranks in importance approaching that of the Dust Bowl and BPA songs. As he asserts, Guthrie's Beluthahatchee songs—written, arguably, by a white southerner—point

> to what Guthrie learned from Kennedy and how Kennedy's battles and enemies became Guthrie's own. In these lyrics, Guthrie demonstrates his rich encounter with the culture and nature of Kennedy's home state and region. . . . [T]hey represent Guthrie's ability to focus on topics that may be construed as "Southern" in sensibility and

culture at a time in his biography which has generally been over-
looked or regarded, incorrectly, as a period of diminished and fading
creative capacities.[2]

For this reason, the figure of [William] Stetson Kennedy, whom Guthrie
dubbed "Beluthahatchee Bill," looms large in this chapter, as it did in Guthrie's life. The Beluthahatchee period is particularly important, too, for what
it shows us about Guthrie's wrestling with the issue of race in America—and
how far he had come from his early days in Oklahoma and Texas, where he
had not appeared the most racially enlightened of individuals.

Guthrie often looked back at the racism that had driven the politics of his
boyhood in Oklahoma and had been perpetuated even by his father, a supporter of the Ku Klux Klan and an active pamphleteer against social equality
for African Americans. As Guthrie sheepishly reported to Alan Lomax for
the 1940 Library of Congress recordings, in Oklahoma—where it was "about
one fourth Indians, one fourth Negroes and one half white"—they had "some
crazy way . . . of looking at the colored situation."[3] Nine years later, during a
live performance, Guthrie recalled the trickery that had been used to swindle
Native Americans out of their land, once "millions and millions of dollars'
worth of oil pools" had been discovered beneath the Oklahoma soil: "They
used dope, they used opium, they used every kind of a trick to get these Indians to sign over their lands." Black Oklahomans, too, were harshly targeted:

> There used to be a state law in Oklahoma that a white man could not
> marry a Negro nor an Indian. . . . Then after the oil come in and the
> Indians got so rich, our governor passed a new state law that a Negro
> could not marry a white man nor an Indian—but a white man *could*
> marry an Indian. But the white man could not marry a Negro. So
> the poor Negro could not have any state lands.[4]

Such sympathetic awareness from Guthrie could only have come after
his immersion into the progressive circles of Los Angeles, for his own racism
prior to then is a matter of record. Joe Klein has summarized, for instance,
the contents of a mock newspaper, "a blatantly racist document called the
'Santa Monica Examine 'Er'" that Guthrie compiled shortly after his arrival
in 1937: "The cover page was filled with cartoons of clichéd jungle blacks

and it was followed by two pages of gossip columns with jokes like: 'What makes a nigger's feet fly the fastes'? Answer: A uniform.'"[5] As Peter La Chapelle notes, following other embarrassing events, such as a public upbraiding for playing a minstrel song called "Run, Nigger, Run" on his KFVD radio program, Guthrie—having absorbed "the racial egalitarianism preached by some quarters of the California Left"—turned a volte-face, becoming "an advocate for racial tolerance by speaking out against Jim Crow restrictions, writing and performing antilynching songs, and, in the *People's World*, defending black jazz against modernist critics."[6]

Guthrie's antiracism came to the fore during the war years, when he declared that the "disease called Jim Crow" was "as bad if not worse than the cancer. But now we're fighting a war to kill every trace of this plague called White (or any other color) Supremacy. Jim Crow and Fascism are one and the same vine."[7] Eventually he became preoccupied with the fictions of racial purity that had driven not only Nazism but also American segregation—particularly the southern brand, with its obsessional defense of white female virginity. The majority of his pronouncements on this topic appear to have come out of an intense period of reflection between November 1952, while at Topanga Canyon, California, and June 1953, when he was camping out at Beluthahatchee. At Topanga he crafted a mock sermon on "Southern White Wombanhood," ostensibly delivered by a hell-fire southern preacher—replete with the characteristic puns, rhymes, and other forms of wordplay that marked the best of his talking blues:

> Folks, howdy, howdy . . .
> We come here today
> Not just to tell one another hello and howdy but to protect
>   something which we've been taught is high and holy and just about
>   as holy as it is high;
> That something brethrens and sistrens, is wombanhood . . .
> And not just white wombanhood, but Southern, southern white womb-
>   anhood, southern womban's whitehood, you could call it.

The deftness with which Guthrie connected the protection of southern white virginity with the depredations of the white-hooded Ku Klux Klan could surely not be lost on the "congregation" ("Under this hood of the south you nearly always find a womban of / some sort and kind"). He thanks his flock for gathering "here to hear me froth at my mouth abouth this thing / called southern white wombanhood":

> Southern white womban hood is the best; southern white womb-
> anhood stands the test. Dont ask me which test. Just
> best by test if you dont use the test which is best.
> Southern white wombanhood is always on the up & come; mostly
> on the come line.[8]

At Beluthahatchee, Guthrie went on to launch into a series of pithy dismissals of the pure "southern white" identity, designed to show up the racial mirage for all it was worth. He derided the whole concept of "southern whiteness" through a raft of absurd associations:

> That big north sea flood they had over in England last week was purely white southern I'ma bettin ya[9]

> That floody bloody river that riz up and warshed old Kansas City on offa this global map must of been a pure southern white flood of some kind[10]

> Them big cyclones is all southern white to be right real truthful[.][11]

And yet, under the circumstances, there still were some things that Guthrie *could* identify conclusively as "southern white"—the "handmade bomb" that had destroyed the house of a black family named Moore;[12] "Everything down south . . . except those dead bodies hung around";[13] and, above all, the Grim Reaper: "Death its very self is southern white."[14]

Allied to Guthrie's contempt for the fictions of racial purity was his sustained advocacy for integration in both social and biological terms—an advocacy fully expressed, for instance, in his condemnations of the color line imposed by his landlord, Fred C. Trump—father of Donald—during his residency at the Beach Haven apartment complex in Brooklyn from 1950 to 1952.[15] By the time he moved into Beach Haven, Guthrie had already witnessed enough of the racism that had turned even the sidewalks of his beloved Coney Island into avenues of the outcast:

I watched your black feet
scuffle down along my
Mermaid Avenue sidewalks
tonight and a thing come
over my mind and said your
ten toenails have all
been looking glasses
full of your hurt face. . . .

I asked that sidewalk why
do people all of your
same color stand along
my curb in the fronts
of my little stores and
wait for my filthiest
jobs at slow money?

I hate this fascist hat
that puts you down and
keeps you here scuffling.[16]

So much for the war against Hitler that was to have "settle[d] the score once and for all, of all kinds of race-hate."[17] Less than two years into his residency at Beach Haven, Guthrie was damning the restrictive covenants that had kept the Trump complex a virtual all-white ghetto—except for those not-quite-white others, such as East European Jews, would could "pass" in comparison with blacks and other, darker minorities. Indeed, Guthrie looked to Beach Haven's Jewish residents as natural allies in his hopes of smashing Trump's color line—a vision wholly in keeping with his euphoric predictions of the world following the defeat of Nazism and fascism:

This old Jewish looking mother here walking back from the
appetizer store with her sacks full of bagels and loxes
and onion rolls and the morning's morning in your eyes,
you wouldn't care, would you, mother, if your eyes looked

up in these windows of every apartment and saw a sight
a hundred times more alive and living and as funhaving
and as colorstruck as Beach Haven could be.[18]

And for his landlord, he had some particularly harsh words:

> I suppose
> Old Man Trump knows
> How many drops
> Of sad tears
> And crazy fears
> He caused my family
> In and out of
> Beach Haven to feel
> And to fall heir to.[19]

It was at Beach Haven that Guthrie began increasingly to envision fantasies of race mixing, not so much out of any crude desire "on the come line"
but more as an expression of social resistance (if not revolution)—hence one
of the erotic moments he imagined between a young black woman and her
lover, also black, both presumably barred from Beach Haven by Trump's
racist policies. In Guthrie's vision, the color line of biology is erased, just as
he would wish to see it erased in society:

> His finger is my own
> His blackskin hand is my own
> His hours of touch for you are my own
> Because my skin is light and because my
> blood beats Spanish and my breath burns Indian and my
> soul boils negro like your sweet own.[20]

Thus, while Arévalo Mateus proposes, quite plausibly, that Stetson
Kennedy's "affinity" for Guthrie was, "in part, based on seeing in Guthrie a
sufficient degree of the 'Okie,'" the poor white southerner who was a "close
kin" to the "crackers" of Georgia and Florida, Guthrie himself maintained
that his own interest in the people of Kennedy's region was based on their
racial admixture.[21] As he wrote to Kennedy in August 1950:

I always did feel a curious kind of a hot sympathy for your peoples
down in there . . . because it was out of your state that lots of my
Indian tribes and negro slaves and runaways of all (lighter colors)
came over to . . . go down somewhere along the muddy bogs or the
dry sandy gulches or the hot gravely canyons or the stickery weed
patches of my own natural born and native state called Oklahoma.
Lots of my tribes did come up out of your palmetto muds as I see in
your book *Palmetto Country*.[22]

It is more than significant that the majority of Guthrie's attacks on the
defenders of white racial purity were written at Kennedy's Beluthahatchee
in 1953. As Guthrie wrote in a notebook missive addressed to none other
than Harriet Tubman, Kennedy's refuge was the "fifty acre patch of wild
waters and wild trees and wild roots and wild leaves which a wilder gang of
hoodlum hooded KKK neighborfolks tried to chop, to hack, to rip, to blast,

Stetson Kennedy, 1946. Photographer unknown. Courtesy of the Stetson Kennedy
Trust, care of the Stetson Kennedy Foundation: www.StetsonKennedy.com.

to wreck, to smash all to smithereens."[23] The Klan had had ample reason to target Kennedy (besides his dilution of the pure white bloodline through his marriage to a mixed-race Cuban). In the 1940s he had infiltrated their organization, rising to the high rank of "kleagle," an adventure recounted on Kennedy's website prior to his death in 2011: "While undercover in the Klan, he provided information—including secret code words and details of Klan rituals—to the writers of the *Superman* radio program, resulting in a series of four episodes in which Superman battled the KKK. . . . America's kids were sharing the most current secretive Ku Klux Klan passwords as fast as the KKK Grand Dragon could create them." Thanks to Kennedy, too, "for a time in the 1940s, Washington news commentator Drew Pearson was reading Klan meeting minutes on national radio."[24] And if the Florida Klan members were too dense to know that Kennedy and his colleague in the infiltration, the appropriately named John Brown, had blown their cover, they could read about it in Kennedy's exposés, *I Rode with the Ku Klux Klan* (1942)—subsequently republished under the title, *The Klan Unmasked* (1956)—and *Southern Exposure* (1946).

In 1942 Kennedy had published his first book, *Palmetto Country,* in the American Folkways Series edited by Erskine Caldwell. This document of Florida folklore was—in the tradition of his fellow collectors John and Alan Lomax—the result of Kennedy's travels throughout the state with his protégé, Zora Neale Hurston, during which they recorded the "songs, tales, and anecdotes of pogey fishermen at May port, railroad gandy-dancers, Latin cigar makers, Greek spongers, and turpentiners"; Kennedy had called it "a sort of barefoot social history of Florida."[25] Shortly after its publication, he received a letter scrawled on the back of the book's dust jacket, written by his new fan, Woody Guthrie: "I don't know of a book on my whole shelf that hits me any harder than your *Palmetto Country.* It gives me a better trip and taste and look and feel for Florida than I got in the forty-seven states I've actually been in body and tramped in boot. If only, and if only, all our library books could say what you did—the jokes and songs and old ballads about voodoo and the hoodoo and the bigly winds down in your neck of the woodvine."[26] This was the start of a firm friendship based on a progressive, antifascist worldview shared by two unique individuals who had traveled on significant journeys—Guthrie, the casual Oklahoma racist who had long been working to educate himself out of his racism, and Kennedy, who had gone into the bowels of Floridian terror, driven not only by a life-threatening double agency but also a sense of macabre humor in the face of both the danger and the absurdities of Jim Crow in the South.

After Kennedy, with knowing quixotism, "announced himself as a 'color-blind' candidate" for the Florida Senate in 1950 (as he recalled in the third person), "a delegation of Klansmen attended his meetings, and the Grand Dragon passed the word around that Kennedy's 'head would be blown off' if he continued to speak. The Klan did set fire to Kennedy's property, and on election day he was arrested and threatened with lynching."[27] As Diane Roberts notes, "His opponent was Democrat George Smathers, the choice of Big Business and white supremacy. Smathers had money and the party machine behind him"—as well as the powerful backing of the Du Pont family. "Kennedy had pretty much nothing but a campaign song by that 'red' Woody Guthrie, which Florida radio stations refused to play."[28] Indeed, the song—a talking blues—remained uncovered until it was recorded by Billy Bragg and Wilco for the *Mermaid Avenue* sessions:

> I done spent my last three cents
> Mailing my letter to the president.
> I didn't make a show, I didn't make a dent,
> So I'm swinging over to this independent gent.
> Stetson Kennedy. Writing his name in.
>
> I cain't win out to save my soul
> Long as Smathers-Dupont's got me in the hole.
> Them war profit boys are squawkin' and balkin.'
> That's what's got me out here walkin' and talkin.'
> Knocking on doors and windows.
> Wake up and run down election morning
> And scribble in Stetson Kennedy.[29]

Likewise, in "Beluthahatchee Bill," Guthrie applauded Kennedy's bravery in the face of Klan terror, after the hooded marauders had repeatedly attacked his ranch. Guthrie himself had purportedly been witness to one attack in 1951. As Ed Cray describes it,

Guthrie had arrived in Florida in time to reinforce a motley platoon of neighbors Kennedy had assembled to defend Beluthahatchee. Anticipating a raid by the local klavern, Guthrie visited a local gunshop and had made cartridges for Kennedy's rifle, a World War I vintage Springfield '03. . . .

When the klan finally roared up in a convoy of pickup trucks Kennedy's impromptu platoon was at the ready. Guthrie, at the first alarm, tumbled from his hammock. In his excitement he dashed across the hot coals in the barbecue pit, Springfield in hand, to blaze away at the marauding night riders. Amid the gunfire and a hail of falling twigs and leaves, the panicked klansmen circled the driveway in front of Kennedy's home and sped off, never to return.[30]

Joe Klein presents this particular episode as a practical joke on Guthrie engineered by Kennedy himself,[31] but in any event, other Klan attacks were very real and they ultimately succeeded in driving Kennedy and his wife from Beluthahatchee for a time. As the Florida historian Gary Mormino observed, "Stetson Kennedy is lucky to be alive. . . . He was one of the most hated men in America."[32] That is surely one reason why Guthrie liked him so much, as he makes clear in his ode to one of the Klan's greatest nemeses:

> Name that I was borned with, name that I've got still,
> Rings out by the sound of Beluthahatchee Bill;
> You Kluxers tried to scare me, with your words of swill,
> But you'll never scare me none, not Beluthahatchee Bill.
> Beluthahatchee Bill, old Beluthahatchee Bill,
> Freedom-lovin', freedom-huntin', easy-ridin' Bill;
> You can swing me and hang me, and beat me to your fill,
> But you'll never slack my speed none, not Beluthahatchee Bill.[33]

It would be impossible to determine precisely how Kennedy's fearlessness, his example of interracial love in the face of terror, his humor, and his quixotism might have influenced Guthrie. But in Kennedy's celebrated mock guidebook, *The Jim Crow Guide to the USA*—published by Jean-Paul Sartre in 1956 after no American publisher would touch it—one can appreciate both the cultural and judicial contexts that would indeed have prompted

Guthrie to agitate for interracial engagement, both public and private, on a grand scale. Kennedy's justification for the *Jim Crow Guide,* as stated in its Preface, was that "other guides" to the United States, "irresponsibly recommending hotels, restaurants, tours, entertainment, and so on, without taking into account the existing taboos, can actually get you killed."[34] The book is written as though Berlitz had set out to inform the intrepid traveler how not to anger the natives of a notoriously backward society. Thus, such helpful chapter headings as "Who May Marry Whom," "Who May Live Where," and "Who May Travel How" reveal with deadpan calm the official and unofficial codes of American apartheid that predated those of South Africa.

It was an apartheid that Guthrie knew all too well, and that he tried to capture in many of his Beluthahatchee songs, such as "Pineytimber Blues," sung from the point of view of a poor Georgian or Floridian black man defeated by the backbreaking labor of the pine woods, the crushing poverty in spite of his hard work, and the racism that keeps him a virtual "slave" at the mercy of the white "bossman":

> Pineytimber, pineytimber, you sap my life away,
> Pineytimber, pineytimber, you sap my life away
> I sap an' drain y'r pinetree an' I caint save two days pay.
>
> Pineytimber takes my muscles and it gives me back my bones,
> Pineytimber takes my muscles and it gives me back my bones,
> Pineytimer chains my leg till I wish I'z dead'n gone.
> [. . . .]
> Come look in my pineywood timbers ta see how my bossman done,
> Come look in my pineywood timbers ta see how my bossman done,
> You c'n see a haffa dozen dead mens roun' the roots of every stump.[35]

Kennedy maintained that the impact on Guthrie of the racism he witnessed in the area around Beluthahatchee had been a matter of high degree. He knew that Guthrie had been amply exposed to racism in other parts of the United States, both North and South: "Woody no doubt had that experience, so that when he came here to Beluthahatchee, Florida, the plantation racist mentality wasn't all that new to him, but the intensity of it and the universality of it, that was new."[36] Most importantly, it was a "mentality" backed up by the laws of many southern states. In the *Jim Crow Guide,* for instance, Kennedy quotes Georgia state representative David C. Jones on race mixing: "To us that is very offensive. . . . Intermarriage produces half breeds, and half breeds are not conducive to the higher type of society. We in the South are a proud and progressive people. Half breeds cannot be proud. In the South, we have pure blood line and we intend to keep it that way" (61).

Crucially, Kennedy pointed out that the facilitation of Jim Crow extended to well north of the Mason-Dixon Line—something upon which Guthrie had already commented in his songs condemning northern miscarriages of justice ("Buoy Bells for Trenton"), the killings of unarmed black men by northern police ("The Ferguson Brothers Killing"), and the racially charged riots against Paul Robeson in Peekskill, New York, in 1949. As the *Jim Crow Guide* warns, "If you are contemplating interracial matrimony, but are a resident of a state which does not permit it, steer clear of Massachusetts and Vermont in choosing a state in which to get married. Although permitting such marriages, these two states may void your marriage if it is shown that your intention was to evade the law of your home state and then return to it" (59). Thus, Kennedy's intention was to present the truly national character of Jim Crow, but there was no doubt that it was at its most intense, in legal terms, in the southern states.

In marrying a nonwhite woman, Kennedy, of course, had broken the laws of Florida that he summarizes in the *Jim Crow Guide:*

Florida

Forbids marriage between whites and anyone having 1/16th or more Negro blood.

Forbids cohabitation between whites and anyone having 1/8th or more Negro blood. . . .

"All persons of different race and opposite sex who habitually occupy the same room at night" shall be deemed guilty of concubinage, and punished. Offenders may be prosecuted at any time within two years following commission of the offense. (64–65)

(Neighboring Georgia was even less fussy: "'It shall be unlawful for a white person to marry anyone except a white person.'—Acts of 1927" [65].)

Kennedy had thus taken on the status of an outlaw—as we have seen, a fellowship held in high symbolic regard by Guthrie. Outlaws were certainly on his mind during his tenure at Beluthahatchee. In one song he wrote there, "Ellis Island Outlaw," he declared outright his own affinity for Kennedy and all other breakers of unjust laws:

> Ellis Island
> Ellis Island
> Ellis Island cant hold us all!
>
> All of us are outlaws, outlaws,
> All of us are outlaws, outlaws,
> All of us are breakers of the big law
> All of us are breakers of the laws.[37]

Woody Guthrie at Beluthahatchee, c. 1953. Photo by Stetson Kennedy. Courtesy of the Woody Guthrie Archives.

From the shores of "Good lake Beluthahatchee" he praised Julius and Ethel Rosenberg, convicted of—and executed for—passing atomic secrets to the Russians (by Guthrie's reasoning, thus ensuring that the United States would never again detonate an atomic bomb). This was, to Guthrie, a brave and patriotic step, to be hailed loud enough for the "bull gators" and the "sweet Florida sundown" itself to hear of it.[38]

In another Beluthahatchee song, "Tuccumcari Striker," a lone woman worker stands up against an entire phalanx of state repression, while in "Pistol Packer," the lone gunman has some strong words for the uniformed enforcers of the corrupt racist laws:

> I'ma pistol packer champion
> I've never yet lost a draw
> I give my gravedigger plenty of work
> With officers of the law.
>
> I'm a rebel soldier gunhand
> My trigger fingers itch
> A dozen tinny badge fools like you
> Have ended in my ditch.
> [. . . . .]
> You c'n blast at me with gassybombs
> And heave me your hand grenades
> I'll send you to join my graveyard gang
> Where I send my good losers like you.
>
> You c'n come at me with yr billysticks
> Your knives and your cold brassy knucks
> The last few dozen that's come at me
> They're pushing my flowers up.[39]

Guthrie recalled with pride, in a letter to his Folkways producer, Moses Asch, all the "fighting Jimmy Crow balladsongs" that he had written "off down in them raceyhate Florida jungles."[40] In an extended free verse poem, linguistically battered by the increasing depredations of Huntington's disease, Guthrie envisaged himself floating "Up & above & out from & over /

This Belutha[ha]tchee Lake . . . & your whole / State called Florida," noting not only "everything your best hand / raises up and builds up down here to work for you," but also that which "holds us all back":

> Get rid of that
> Get rid of that one thing
> Now before one more unborn second flyes past us;
> Get rid of jimmycrow;
> Get rid of racey hate;
> Get rid of that. Get rid of that. Get rid of that.[41]

It was a stance that Guthrie would maintain until his last day on earth. His inexorable descent into the darkening twilight of Huntington's disease did nothing to undermine his commitment to racial justice and the elimination of race hatred, a manifestation of the fascism that he, his guitar, and his pen were pledged to kill.

CONCLUSION
DOWN OR UP OR ANYWHERE

When Guthrie reflected on his journeys into the heart of the Jim Crow South, as well as many other places, he found himself coming back to Einstein, who had proved to him "that there ain't no such thing as east west north or south." Einstein seemed to imply that, Beluthahatchee and the southern state codes notwithstanding, distinctions of place were merely relative:

> It seems to me like the farther down south you get the worse you see the colored races treated. But, when I say down south what do I mean, south of where, south of what, south of which? Well, the colored folks get treated just as bad up north, and just as miserable out west, and lots more of both back east.
>
> This is because we stand around and let them draw all kinds of crazy boundary lines in between us and betwixt us. Somebody way up in a big high office has drawed a boundary line around every one of us and it keeps all of us cut off apart.
>
> Einstein chopped down all of these crazy boundary lines for the next forty-nine billion trillion centuries to roll.[1]

Well, if only. Guthrie himself had proved through his voluminous writing that place was indeed important—as important as time. This was the double-bind in which he was caught: on the one hand, he wished in a utopian sense to be released from the limitations of place, seeing the world as just "a little rubber ball" in space, where the lines of division—whether of class, race, or region—could be held up as the fictions he felt them to be. His late writings in particular reflect a positive yearning to be uncoupled from the chains of the three-dimensional world. His "Einstein Theme Song" concludes with the verses he wrote for his hero—"a theme song, Mr. Einstein, for you to sing when you saw your fiddle at your lectures":

> If I cain't go east nor west,
> If I can't go north nor south,
> I can still go in and out,
> I can still go round and around;
> And around and around and around
> And around and around and around
> I can still go in and out
> And around and around and around.[2]

He would die, he knew, and his spirit (if such a thing existed after death) could go "down or up or anywhere"; he wouldn't care, as long as his "scribbling might stay."[3]

But even if his "scribbling" stayed, there could be no telling where it might be picked up and taken. Guthrie was aware that his art shared the same fluidity—the same potential "deterritorialization"—as that of countless other songwriters throughout history, known and unknown. He recalled once singing his version of an old English folk song, "Dream of a Miner's Child": "I thought I was singing a new song myself, but an old Swedish miner in Butte, Montana heard me in a saloon singing with my hat on the floor for tips. He said, 'I heard that song, or its twin sister, one or the other, over a half a century ago, in Wales.'"[4] Songs "will travel," Guthrie said (in the spirit of Joe Hill), "and [that] is better than a great sermon that everybody forgets."[5] Territory and region, he seemed to imply, were ultimately insignificant, at least for folksingers: "It ain't no surprise to find mountaineers, swamp dwellers, desert people, and dustbowlers of all colors, making up and singing some of the best of our American sea songs. Either there is a shot of the sea in their history, or a touch of the sea in their hopes."[6]

And yet—down, up, east, west, California, New York: all were indeed formative places for Guthrie, fashioning his experiences and contributing their imagery to his songs. "Dustbowlers" might well write sea songs and sailors might well write Dust Bowl ballads, but one of the enduring impressions coming out of Guthrie's art is not only that he was "there" in the Whitmanian sense—the bardic sense—but also that he was "there" on the ground, whether "there" meant the Dust Bowl, the road, California, the Pacific Northwest, New York, or the Jim Crow South (as well as on a ship at sea). Not for nothing did Guthrie—ever the wanderer until his body gave out—refer to himself as "a compass-pointer man."[7] Guthrie's "compass" pointed to particular locations, each one providing a definitive chapter in his life and a peculiar cast to his overall body of work.

But even when Guthrie had only been "there" in the bardic sense, it was his capacity to listen and to transform that made others' experiences seem like his own. Guy Logsdon and Jeff Place have written of his ability to turn the "stories, problems, aspirations, tragedies, loves, and work experiences" of unknown and formerly unsung people "into first-person narratives that still evoke emotional responses from those who read and listen."[8] Or, as Martin Butler observes, out of Guthrie's "communal 'we'" comes "a communal 'I.'"[9] Guthrie himself admitted as much:

> I have heard a storm of words in me, enough to write several hundred songs and that many books. I know that these words I hear are not my own private property.
>
> I borrowed them from you, the same as I walked through the high winds and borrowed enough air to keep me moving. I borrowed enough to eat and drink and to keep me alive. I borrowed the shirt you made, the coat you spun, the underwear you fixed, and those socks you wove.[10]

Guthrie's terms of reference here, with the suggested corporeality of eating and drinking and clothing, reflect the artist's sleight of hand. This is the work of the bardic "there" against the raw demands of the physical presence, the occupation of space. Guthrie was, of course, not physically "there" to borrow anyone's shirt or coat or underwear or socks. But it is in the genius of his songs that he has been able convince millions otherwise, well into the twenty-first century, long after his spirit has pointed its own compass toward the "down or up or anywhere" to which it has gone. In mapping Woody Guthrie, we have attempted to accomplish what can only be an unfinished task. It still remains for us to listen, and listen, and listen again.

CHRONOLOGY

1912   Woodrow Wilson Guthrie is born on July 14 to Charlie and Nora Belle Guthrie in Okemah, Oklahoma. He has two older siblings, Clara and Roy.

1918   Woody's younger brother, George, is born.

1919   Woody's fourteen-year-old sister, Clara, is fatally burned in a coal-oil fire.

1920   Economic slump hits Oklahoma. Charlie Guthrie's tenants begin to default on their mortgages. Within a year, Charlie Guthrie, too, is broke.

Oil is discovered beneath Spring Hill, nine miles from Okemah. Other local oil discoveries follow; Charlie Guthrie's fortunes begin to revive.

1922   Woody's sister Mary Jo is born.

1923   Due to the oil boom, Okemah's population jumps from roughly two thousand to fifteen thousand. In spite of the boom, Charlie Guthrie is soon bankrupt. The Guthries move briefly to Oklahoma City, where Charlie delivers groceries and sells fire extinguishers door to door.

1924   The Guthries return to a run-down section of Okemah. About this time, Woody begins to learn the harmonica, imitating the whistle of the freight trains as taught to him by a local black musician named George. Woody develops his craft at cartooning.

1927   Charlie loses his job as an auto license clerk.

Charlie is almost fatally burned in a coal-oil fire, possibly started by Nora Belle, suffering from the ravages of Huntington's disease. Nora Belle is committed to the Central State Hospital in Norman, Oklahoma. Charlie moves to Pampa, Texas, while Woody remains with Roy in Okemah. He lives with a series of Okemah families until 1929.

1929   Woody's first hobo experience, traveling through Houston to the Gulf of Mexico and back.

After returning to Okemah, Woody moves to Pampa to help Charlie run a boomtown flophouse. He gets a job at Shorty Harris's Drug Store, where he begins to learn the guitar from Carter Family records. He drops out of high school and becomes a sign painter.

Nora Belle dies in the Central State Hospital.

1930   Woody forms his first country music band, the Corn Cob Trio, with friends Matt Jennings and Cluster Baker. They begin playing at markets and barn dances across Texas, as well as on local radio stations.

1933   Woody marries Matt Jennings's sister, Mary.

1934   Woody writes what he later declares his first song: "Old Gray Team of Horses," about the intrusion of modernity into a rural backwater, signaled by the arrival a Ford car.

1935   Woody briefly advertises his own faith healing (or "Trouble Busting") business in the local papers.

"Black Sunday": the worst of the dust storms hit Pampa on Palm Sunday, April 14. Woody writes the first of his Dust Bowl ballads, "The Great Dust Storm" and "Dusty Old Dust" ("So Long, It's Been Good to Know Yuh").

Woody and Mary's first child, Gwendolyn, is born. She will die from Huntington's disease at the age of forty-one.

1936   Woody drifts around Texas, Arkansas, Oklahoma, Arizona, and as far as California, looking for odd jobs. With the roads flooded with indigent hitchhikers, he resorts to his most concerted period of freight-hopping.

1937   Woody heads west again, hitchhiking and walking to California. He hooks up with his cousin Leon "Oklahoma Jack" Guthrie; they form a country music band in hopes of capitalizing on the current "singing cowboy" craze in Hollywood.

Woody and Jack secure a radio show on KFVD radio in Los Angeles, eventually joined by Maxine "Lefty Lou" Crissman. Jack soon leaves the trio. Back in Pampa, Woody and Mary's second child, Carolyn Sue, is born. Like her sister, she will succumb to Huntington's disease at the age of forty-one.

Woody is joined by Mary and the children, and they move to Glendale, California.

1938   Woody and Lefty Lou spend a brief time broadcasting on XELO radio in Tijuana, Mexico. They quit over issues of censorship and management interference. They resume their KFVD broadcasting.

Lefty Lou quits show business because of ill health. Woody's radio manager, J. Frank Burke—also a newspaper editor—commissions Woody to report on conditions in the Dust Bowl migrant camps in California. Woody spends five months in the camps and Hoovervilles, telephoning in his reports.

1939   Woody meets Ed Robbin, the Los Angeles correspondent for the *People's World,* the Communist Party daily. Robbin introduces Woody to the paper's editor, Al Richmond, who offers him a column and cartooning opportunities. Robbin secures performances for Woody at progressive, union, and Communist Party events.

Woody launches his "Woody Sez" column for the *People's World.*

Robbin introduces Woody to actor and activist Will Geer, who becomes one of his most influential Popular Front mentors.

Woody's son, Bill, is born. He will die in a car crash at the age of twenty-three.

Woody breaks with Frank Burke over the Hitler-Stalin Pact and loses his job at KFVD. The Guthries return to Pampa.

1940   At the suggestion of Will Geer, Woody relocates to New York City. Geer introduces Woody to Alan Lomax.

Woody writes "God Blessed America," subsequently retitled "This Land Is Your Land."

Woody meets Pete Seeger, Lead Belly, and other prominent folksingers at a "Grapes of Wrath" benefit organized by Geer and Lomax. Lomax later dates the "renaissance of American folk music" from this meeting on March 3.

Celebrated cartoonist Art Shields praises Woody in his *Daily Worker* column. Within the week, the *Worker* is printing the "Woody Sez" columns.

Woody records at the Library of Congress for Lomax.

Woody's first New York radio broadcast on Lomax's *Columbia School of the Air* program for CBS. He appears shortly afterward on Norman Corwin's *Pursuit of Happiness* program (CBS).

Woody records *Dust Bowl Ballads* for RCA Victor.

On the way to Pampa to see Mary and the children, Woody stops in Washington, DC, with Lomax and Pete Seeger, where they begin work on the radical song collection *Hard Hitting Songs for Hard-Hit People*. Woody and Seeger travel together through the South.

Woody makes his first appearance on CBS radio's *Back Where I Come From*, directed by future film auteur Nicholas Ray. A raft of commercial network appearances follow: *We the People* (CBS/ Sanka); *Cavalcade of America* (NBC/DuPont) and *Pipe Smoking Time* (CBS/Model Tobacco).

Possibly in fear of his commercial contracts, Woody ceases writing his "Woody Sez" column for the *Daily Worker*. He quits *Back Where I Come From* after arguing with Nicholas Ray.

Woody quits his *Pipe Smoking Time* show over censorship. He meets Lee Hays and Millard Lampell, whom he will join, along with Seeger, in the Almanac Singers.

1941   Woody turns his back on New York broadcasting and heads for Los Angeles with his family. He is briefly allowed back on KFVD, but not for pay. The Guthries live indigently for three months north of Los Angeles, in the High Sierras, and the foothills; Woody paints signs and cuts and hauls timber to make ends meet.

The Guthries are rescued from destitution by the arrival of an invitation from the Bonneville Power Authority (BPA) for Woody to write songs in praise of the Grand Coulee Dam. He travels to Portland, Oregon, is hired as "information consultant" for the BPA, and writes twenty-six songs in the space of a month.

Unbeknownst to Woody, the paid informer Hazel Huffman names him as a communist before the Dies Committee in Congress. The FBI opens a surveillance file on him.

His BPA contract over in June, Woody returns alone to New York. Mary returns with the children to Pampa and soon files for divorce.

Celebrated Martha Graham dancer Sophie Maslow choreographs *Dust Bowl Ballads*.

Woody records two albums with the Almanac Singers (*Deep Sea Shanties* and *Sod Buster Ballads*) and joins them on a coast-to-coast tour in aid of the Congress of Industrial Organizations (CIO).

Woody and the other Almanac Singers establish their first "Almanac House" in Greenwich Village, New York. Woody begins working on *Bound for Glory*.

A German U-boat sinks the USS *Reuben James* off Iceland in October. Woody and the Almanacs write "The Sinking of the Reuben James."

After the Japanese attack on Pearl Harbor, the Almanacs commit themselves to writing pro-war songs.

1942   Sophie Maslow begins rehearsing *Folksay*, with Woody as a live performer. Here he meets Maslow's dance colleague Marjorie Mazia, who will become his second wife.

The Almanacs perform major network radio shows, enjoying brief status as one of the country's most popular war propaganda acts, until the press outs them as communists—"Stalin's songbirds." The group soon falls apart.

Woody signs book contract with E. P. Dutton for *Bound for Glory*.

Marjorie, still married to Joseph Mazia, learns that she is pregnant with Woody's child. She remains with her husband in Philadelphia until after the baby's birth.

Woody appears on the Office of War Information radio programs, *Labor for Victory* and *Jazz in America*. The sign "This Machine Kills Fascists" makes its first appearance on his guitar.

1943   Woody and Marjorie's first daughter, Cathy Ann, is born in February.

Bound for Glory is published to strong notices in the press and on radio.

Marjorie and Cathy join Woody in New York.

Heading off his army induction notice, Woody joins the merchant marine with Cisco Houston and Jim Longhi. Aboard ship, Woody confesses to Longhi and Cisco his fear that he may have inherited his mother's illness.

Woody's ship docks in Palermo, Sicily. The inseparable trio—Woody, Cisco, and Longhi, whom Woody dubs "the Seamen Three"—explore war-torn Sicily.

Woody's ship sails to Tunis and is mined in Bizerte Harbor. The Seamen Three explore parts of Tunisia together.

Home between voyages, Woody, Marjorie, and Cathy move to Mermaid Avenue in Coney Island. Marjorie teaches dance while Woody remains home to care for Cathy.

Woody receives a second army induction notice and returns to the merchant marine.

1944   Woody's ship sails to North Africa and docks in Oran. The Seamen Three explore parts of Algeria.

Woody returns home to New York, where he records Lomax's radio ballad opera *The Martins and the Coys*.

Woody meets Moses Asch and begins six weeks' recording for him with Cisco Houston. The Asch recordings are later named by the Smithsonian's Jeff Place as "the mother lode . . . the bulk of Guthrie's recorded legacy."

A third draft notice leads to Woody's final tour with the merchant marine.

An acoustic mine cripples Woody's ship just off Omaha Beach, Normandy. The ship is towed to Southampton; Woody explores bombed-out London and appears on the BBC's *Children's Hour* radio program.

Woody arrives back home in New York. He tours the East Coast with the "Roosevelt Bandwagon" in support of FDR's third reelection campaign.

First episode of Woody's WNEW radio show, *Ballad Gazette*, which he introduces with "This Land Is Your Land." The show lasts twelve weeks before Woody breaks with the network over censorship.

1945   Woody's Asch/Stinson album, *Folksay*, is released. It is his first solo album since *Dust Bowl Ballads*.

Woody receives a fourth draft notice and hopes for a fourth tour with the merchant marine, but with his seaman's papers revoked by the Office of Naval Intelligence because of his communist associations, he is inducted into the US Army and sent to a series of basic training camps in New Jersey, Texas, and Illinois. He trains as a teletype operator.

After the destruction of Hiroshima and Nagasaki, Woody writes songs celebrating the work of the atomic bomb in ending the war against Japan.

Woody marries Marjorie while on furlough. He is sent to a Las Vegas air base to await demobilization.

Upon his army discharge in December, Woody begins a fitful period of child care, but outnumbering his letters and notebook entries expressing frustration are the jottings that he would turn into some of his most renowned children's songs.

Woody learns that his cousin "Oklahoma Jack" Guthrie has recorded his song "Oklahoma Hills" and has claimed authorship. After negotiation, the two are named as joint composers, although the song was written by Woody alone.

1946   Pete Seeger and colleagues launch People's Songs Inc., with Woody on the board of directors.

Asch commissions Woody to write an album of songs honoring the labor martyrs Sacco and Vanzetti. After many false starts, the album will finally appear in 1964. Woody begins recording his children's songs for Asch. They will appear on two albums: *Songs to Grow On: Nursery Days* and *Songs to Grow On: Work Songs for Nursery Days*.

With his Huntington's disease further entrenched and mistaken for alcoholism, Woody and Marjorie consider regular periods of separation in order the save their marriage. He begins writing his novel *House of Earth*, which will be published posthumously in 2013.

1947   Woody and Marjorie's daughter, Cathy Ann, dies in an electrical fire on February 10.

Woody and Marjorie's second child, Arlo, is born in July.

Woody finishes writing his second autobiographical novel, *Study Butte*, which will be published posthumously in 1976 as *Seeds of Man*.

1948   A plane carrying twenty-eight unnamed Mexican migrant workers crashes in the Los Gatos Canyon in California, prompting Woody to write the poetic ode "Deportee." It will be set to music in the 1950s by Martin Hoffman, becoming one of Woody's most popular songs. Not until 2013 would a memorial to the lost migrants be erected, bearing all their names as recovered by the writer Tim Z. Hernandez.

Amid considerable marital tension and separations, Woody and Marjorie's third child, Joady, is born in December.

1949   People's Songs Inc. dissolves against the backdrop of anticommunist purges in the CIO and the intensifying Cold War.

Woody witnesses the antiblack, anti-Semitic violence of the Peekskill Riots against Paul Robeson and writes twenty-one songs about them.

1950   Woody and Marjorie's fourth child, Nora, is born in January while Woody sits in jail for vagrancy.

The Korean War begins, prompting about fifty songs from Woody between 1950 and 1953.

The Weavers and Gordon Jenkins record a version of Woody's song "So Long, It's Been Good to Know Yuh," which earns Woody the single largest royalty advance he will ever receive: ten thousand dollars, with which Marjorie can open the Marjorie Mazia School of Dance.

The royalty advance also enables the Guthries to move into larger premises at Beach Haven, Brooklyn, where Woody will soon write a series of tirades against his landlord, Fred C. Trump (father of the future US president), in protest against racist rental policies.

The publisher Howie Richmond agrees to publish Woody's songs in a series of school songbooks. Through this strategy, "This Land Is Your Land" and other Guthrie songs earn their first popularity.

1951   Woody is hospitalized in Coney Island for a ruptured appendix. He is visited by Elliot Charles Adnopoz—the future "Ramblin' Jack Elliott"—who shortly afterward virtually joins the Guthrie household for a year and a half.

Woody travels to Florida to visit Stetson Kennedy. Upon his return, Marjorie refuses to have him back, worried for the children's safety as his behavior becomes more erratic and unpredictable. He wanders around New York City and elsewhere for months, finally taking a room on Fourteenth Street in Manhattan.

1952   In spite of the Red Scare and his deepening illness, Woody manages to secure a recording contract for Decca on the strength of the Weavers' recording of "So Long, It's Been Good to Know Yuh." Woody's final commercial recording session is severely marred by his illness. The Decca record is never released.

Still unaware that Huntington's disease is at the root of his behavior, Woody checks in to an alcoholics' detox program at Kings County Hospital. A month later, he voluntarily commits himself to the psychiatric ward at Bellevue Hospital after a halfhearted suicide threat. He is wrongly diagnosed as a schizophrenic and slated for shock treatment. In his writing, he increasingly makes associations between his own personal breakdown and that of modern American society at large.

After a return to the detox program at Kings County Hospital, Woody is transferred to Brooklyn State Hospital for two months' evaluation and insulin shock treatment. The admitting doctors conclude he shows "elements of schizophrenia, psychopathy and psychoneurotic anxiety state, not to mention the mental and personality changes occurring in Huntington's chorea."

A neurologist conclusively diagnoses Woody with Huntington's chorea. Upon his discharge from the hospital, Woody flees to Will Geer's artists' community at Topanga Canyon, Los Angeles, to come to terms with his disease.

1953   At Topanga, Woody meets the young, married Anneke Van Kirk Marshall, and they begin an affair. They travel together to New York, meet up with Jack Elliott (with his Model A Ford), and drive to the Stetson Kennedy ranch at Beluthahatchee, where they spend six months. Woody writes a body of songs against Jim Crow racism as well as a surreal play called *Skybally.*

Woody severely burns his right arm in a campfire at Beluthahatchee, virtually putting an end to his guitar playing.

Woody and Anneke return by bus to Topanga via Juarez, where Woody files for divorce from Marjorie. Anneke learns she is pregnant with Woody's child.

Woody and Anneke marry in Los Angeles.

1954   Woody and Anneke return to New York City and take an apartment on West Fifth Street. Woody's final recording session for Asch—with Jack Elliott, Sonny Terry, and Brownie McGhee—is a shambles.

Woody and Anneke's daughter, Lorina Lynn, is born. She will die in a car crash at the age of nineteen.

With his third marriage crumbling under the strains of his illness, Woody drives with Jack Elliott to San Diego. They hop a freight to Los Angeles and stay in Topanga for a time before Woody lights out alone for Washington State, where he spends a night in jail for vagrancy. After nights in jail in British Columbia and Montana, he drifts to Denver, El Paso, Tulsa, and Columbus, Ohio, where the local paper publishes a profile: "City Prison Houses Distinguished Author and Composer—And Hobo."

Upon his return to New York, Woody checks himself into Brooklyn State Hospital and increasingly writes of Jesus as his savior and his "best doctor." The FBI take him off their surveillance list, citing his illness and lack of evidence of Communist Party membership.

After months of increasing distance, Anneke files for divorce.

1956   Woody's friends organize a Woody Guthrie tribute concert at New York's Pythian Hall on March 17 to raise money for the Guthrie Children's Trust Fund. Folk music scholars will later mark this as the beginning of Woody's "canonization."

Woody checks himself out of Brooklyn State Hospital. After a few days of aimless wandering through Brooklyn and New Jersey, he is picked up for vagrancy and committed to the Greystone Park Psychiatric Hospital in Morris Plains. Marjorie and the children make regular visits to him there.

The Greystone Park doctors reaffirm the September 1952 diagnosis of Huntington's disease ("Huntington's Chorea with psychotic reaction"), altering their initial diagnosis of "Schizophrenic Reaction, Paranoid Type."

Woody writes his last letter in December, pleading for his children to visit him once more.

1959   Bob and Sidsel Gleason begin hosting Woody and his growing number of acolytes in their East Orange, New Jersey, apartment on Sundays.

1961   Bob Dylan visits Woody for the first time at the Gleasons' in January. He writes "Song to Woody" immediately afterward.

Marjorie transfers Woody from Greystone Park back to Brooklyn State Hospital. He spends weekends with Marjorie and the children at their home in Howard Beach. About this time, Woody takes Arlo out to their backyard to make sure he knows all the verses to "This Land Is Your Land."

1964   Woody's *Library of Congress Recordings* are issued by Elektra.

1965   The first collection of Woody's writings, *Born to Win*, is published. By now, Woody has stopped speaking altogether, simply blinking once for "yes" and twice for "no."

1966   The US Department of the Interior honors Woody with its Conservation Service Award.

Dr. John Whittier, the Huntington's disease specialist at Creedmoor State Hospital in Queens, takes an interest in Woody's case. He advises Marjorie to have Woody transferred into his care, which she does.

1967   Woody dies in Creedmoor State Hospital on October 3.

Marjorie launches the Committee to Combat Huntington's Disease, which will eventually become the Huntington's Disease Society of America.

NOTES

PREFACE

1. Edward Comentale, *Sweet Air: Modernism, Regionalism, and American Popular Song* (Urbana: University of Illinois Press, 2013), 13.

2. Country Joe McDonald, *Thinking of Woody Guthrie* (Vanguard, 1969).

3. Michael Harrington, *The Other America: Poverty in the United States* (New York: Touchstone, 1997 [1962]).

INTRODUCTION

1. Dave Marsh, notes to Woody Guthrie, "The Atom and Me," in Marsh and Harold Leventhal, eds., *Pastures of Plenty* (New York: HarperPerennial,1990), 244.

2. James Overduin, "Einstein's Spacetime," *Gravity Probe B: Testing Einstein's Universe* (Stanford University), https://einstein.stanford.edu/SPACETIME/spacetime2 .html.

3. Guthrie, "Einstein Brings Back Light Rays," in Robert Shelton, ed., *Born to Win* (New York: Collier, 1967), 193.

4. Guthrie, "Einstein Theme Song," in Shelton, *Born to Win,* 192.

5. David King Dunaway, *How Can I Keep from Singing? The Ballad of Pete Seeger* (New York: Villard Books, 2008), 66.

6. Guthrie, "High Balladree," in Marsh and Leventhal, *Pastures of Plenty,* 22; Guthrie, *Bound for Glory* (New York: E. P. Dutton, 1943), 40.

7. Milton Cantor, *The Divided Left: American Radicalism, 1900–1975* (New York: Hill and Wang, 1978), 24, 31.

8. Guthrie, "How Much, How Long," on *The Live Wire Woody Guthrie* (Mt. Kisco, NY: Woody Guthrie Foundation, 2007), track 1.

9. Guthrie, "If I Was Everything on Earth," as sung by Hans-Eckardt Wenzel on *Ticky Tock* (Contraer Musik, 2003), track 5.

10. Guthrie, "I Was There and the Dust Was There," on *Live Wire Woody Guthrie,* track 3.

11. Dave Marsh, notes to reissue of *Dust Bowl Ballads* (Buddha Records, 2000).

12. Michael Denning, *The Cultural Front: The Laboring of American Culture in the Twentieth Century* (London: Verso, 1998), 3.

13. Denning, *Cultural Front,* 4.

14. Guthrie, quoted in Guy Logsdon, "Introduction," liner notes to Guthrie, *Muleskinner Blues: The Asch Recordings,* Vol. 2 (Smithsonian Folkways, 1999), 11.

15. Robbie Lieberman, *"My Song Is My Weapon": People's Songs, American Communism and the Politics of Culture, 1930–50* (Urbana: University of Illinois Press, 1995), 46.

16. Lieberman, *"My Song Is My Weapon,"* 29.

17. Mike Gold, quoted in R. Serge Denisoff, *Great Day Coming: Folk Music and the American Left* (Baltimore: Penguin, 1973), 38.

18. Richard A. Reuss, with Joanne C. Reuss, *American Folk Music and Left-Wing Politics, 1927–1957* (Lanham, MD: Scarecrow Press, 2000), 74–103; Denisoff, *Great Day Coming,* 16–23.

19. Reuss and Reuss, *American Folk Music,* 96; Lieberman, *"My Song Is My Weapon,"* 34.

20. Library of Congress, *New Deal Programs: Selected Library of Congress Resources,* http://www.loc.gov/rr/program/bib/newdeal/afc.html; Lieberman, *"My Song Is My Weapon,"* 37.

21. Reuss and Reuss, *American Folk Music,* 122, 124.

22. Walt Whitman, "Song of Myself," in *Complete Poetry and Collected Prose,* ed. Justin Kaplan (New York: Literary Classics of the United States, 1982), 64.

CHAPTER 1

1. Donald Worster, *Dust Bowl: The Southern Plains in the 1930s* (Oxford: Oxford University Press, 1982), 49–51.

2. United States House of Representatives, *Investigation of Un-American Propaganda Activities in the United States* (Washington, DC: US Government Publishing Office, 1941), 8463.

3. Woody Guthrie, prefatory remarks to "Boll Weevil Blues," on *Library of Congress Recordings* (Rounder, 1988), disc 1, track 8.

4. Guthrie, prefatory remarks to "Beaumont Rag," on *Library of Congress Recordings,* disc 1, track 5.

5. Guthrie, "My People" (1946), in Shelton, *Born to Win* (New York: Collier, 1967): 215, 217.

6. Although Guthrie indisputably wrote the song himself, he eventually agreed to its copyright under joint authorship with his cousin. See Joe Klein, *Woody Guthrie: A Life* (New York: Delta, 1980), 355.

7. See Arlo Guthrie and the Oklahoma Swing Band, "Oklahoma Hills," on Various Artists, *Woody Guthrie: Hard Travelin'* (Rising Son Records, 2000), track 1.

8. Guthrie, *Bound for Glory,* 209–10.

9. Woody Guthrie, *American Folksong,* ed. Moses Asch (New York: Oak Publications, 1961), 2.

10. E. F. McClanahan, quoted in Garin Burbank, *When Farmers Voted Red: The Gospel of Socialism in the Oklahoma Countryside, 1910–1924* (Westport, CT: Greenwood Press, 1976), 37–38.

11. Ed Cray, *Ramblin' Man: The Life and Times of Woody Guthrie* (New York: Norton, 2004), 10.

12. Woody Guthrie, *Seeds of Man: An Experience Lived and Dreamed* (New York: Pocket Books, 1977), 197.

13. Woody Guthrie, "How Much, How Long," on *The Live Wire Woody Guthrie,* track 1.

14. Guthrie, *Bound for Glory,* 210.

15. Guthrie, *Bound for Glory,* 233.

16. John Gilkas, quoted in Cray, *Ramblin' Man,* 70.

17. Dorothy Sturdivan Kleffman, quoted in Dayton Duncan and Ken Burns, *The Dust Bowl: An Illustrated History* (San Francisco: Chronicle Books, 2012), 56.

18. *Boise City News,* quoted in Duncan and Burns, *Dust Bowl,* 87.

19. Caroline Henderson to Henry A. Wallace, 26 July 1935, in Henderson, *Letters from the Dust Bowl,* ed. Alvin O. Turner (Norman: University of Oklahoma Press, 2001), 142.

20. Guthrie, prefatory remarks to "Boll Weevil Blues," on *Library of Congress Recordings,* disc 1, track 8.

21. Worster, *Dust Bowl,* 24.

22. James M. Gregory, *American Exodus: The Dust Bowl Migration and Okie Culture in California* (New York: Oxford University Press, 1989), 15–16.

23. Guthrie, *Bound for Glory,* 231–32.

24. Guthrie, "The Great Dust Storm (Dust Storm Disaster)," on Guthrie, *Dust Bowl Ballads* (Buddha Records, 2000), track 1.

25. Kurt Vonnegut, quoted in David Standish, "Playboy Interview," *Conversations with Kurt Vonnegut,* ed. William Rodney Allen (Jackson: University Press of Mississippi, 1999), 90–91.

26. Worster, *Dust Bowl,* 5.

27. John Steinbeck, *The Grapes of Wrath* (New York: Penguin, 2002), 33.

28. Dorothy Christenson Williamson, quoted in Duncan and Burns, *Dust Bowl,* 51.

29. Guthrie, "So Long, It's Been Good to Know Yuh," on *Library of Congress Recordings,* disc 1, track 9.

30. Edward P. Comentale, *Sweet Air: Modernism, Regionalism, and American Popular Song* (Urbana: University of Illinois Press, 2013), 150–51.

31. Comentale, *Sweet Air,* 145.

32. Alexander I. Herzen, "A Letter Criticizing *The Bell*'" (1858), in *A Herzen Reader,* ed. and trans. Kathleen Parthé (Evanston, IL: Northwestern University Press, 2012), 69.

33. Denning, *Cultural Front,* 271.

34. Guthrie, "Talking Dust Bowl Blues," on *Dust Bowl Ballads,* track 2.

35. Martin Butler, *Voices of the Down and Out: The Dust Bowl Migration and the Great Depression in the Songs of Woody Guthrie* (Heidelberg: Universitätsverlag Winter, 2007), 88.

36. Hugh W. Foley Jr., "Gray, Otto (and His Oklahoma Cowboys)," *Oklahoma Music Guide II* (Stillwater, OK: New Forums Press, 2014), 298–301.

37. Tony Russell, *Country Music Originals: The Legends and the Lost* (New York: Oxford University Press, 2010), 78.

38. Guthrie, "Dust Pneumonia Blues," on *Dust Bowl Ballads,* track 14.

39. Guthrie, "Dust Pneumonia Blues," on *Library of Congress Recordings,* disc 3, track 4.

40. Albert Camus, "The Myth of Sisyphus" (1942), in *The Myth of Sisyphus and Other Essays* (New York: Vintage, 1991), 121.

41. Guthrie, "Dust Bowl Blues," on *Dust Bowl Ballads,* track 5.

42. Comentale, *Sweet Air,* 149.

43. Guthrie, "Dust Bowl Blues," on *Dust Bowl Ballads,* track 5.

44. Guthrie, "Dust Cain't Kill Me," on *Dust Bowl Ballads,* track 13.

CHAPTER 2

1. Guthrie, prefatory remarks to "So Long, It's Been Good to Know Yuh," *Library of Congress Recordings* (Rounder, 1988), on disc 1, track 9.

2. Gregory, *American Exodus,* 9–10.

3. Denning, *Cultural Front,* 259.

4. See William Stott, *Documentary Expression and Thirties America* (Chicago: University of Chicago Press, 1986).

5. Moses Asch, interview with Guy Logsdon, July 1974, in Logsdon, "Introduction," notes to Guthrie, *Hard Travelin': The Asch Recordings,* vol. 3 (Smithsonian Folkways, 1993).

6. Alan Lomax, introduction to "Lost Train Blues," *Library of Congress Recordings,* disc 1, track 1.

7. Gordon Friesen, in Agnes "Sis" Cunningham and Friesen, *Red Dust and Broadsides: A Joint Biography,* ed. Ronald D. Cohen (Amherst: University of Massachusetts Press, 1999), 224.

8. Jeff Allred, *American Modernism and Depression Documentary* (New York: Oxford University Press, 2009), 10.

9. Guthrie, "Woody, 'The Dustiest of the Dust Bowlers,'" reprinted in Marsh and Leventhal, *Pastures of Plenty,* 41.

10. Guthrie to Marjorie Mazia, October 3, 1945, reprinted in Marsh and Leventhal, *Pastures of Plenty,* 141.

11. Friesen, quoted in Klein, *Woody Guthrie,* 222.

12. Walt Whitman, "Song of Myself," *Complete Poetry and Collected Prose,* ed. Justin Kaplan (New York: Literary Classics of the United States, 1982), 64.

13. Guthrie, "1913 Massacre," on *Hard Travelin': The Asch Recordings,* vol. 3, track 13.

14. Guthrie, "Ludlow Massacre," on *Hard Travelin': The Asch Recordings,* vol. 3, track 20.

15. Guthrie, "Hooversville" (1941), Woody Guthrie Papers: Moses and Frances

Asch Collection, Ralph Rinzler Archives, Center for Folklife and Cultural Heritage, Smithsonian Institution, Washington, DC, Song Texts, box 1, folder 4.

16. Guthrie, prefatory remarks to "California Blues," on *Library of Congress Recordings,* disc 3, track 5.

17. Guthrie, "Woody, 'The Dustiest of the Dust Bowlers,'" reprinted in Marsh and Leventhal, *Pastures of Plenty,* 42.

18. Bess Lomax Hawes, quoted in Cray, *Ramblin' Man,* 231.

19. Archie Green, Preface, *The Big Red Songbook,* ed. Archie Green et al. (Chicago: Charles H. Kerr, 2007), 3.

20. Joe Hill, quoted in Gibbs M. Smith, *Joe Hill* (Layton, UT: Gibbs M. Smith Inc., 1969), 19.

21. Joe Hill, "Casey Jones—The Union Scab," in IWW, *Songs of the Workers to Fan the Flames of Discontent* (Chicago: IWW Publishing Bureau, 1964), 46.

22. Sanford F. Bennett and Joseph P. Webster, "In the Sweet By and By" (1868), *Evening Light Songs* (Guthrie, OK: Faith Publishing House, 1949), 461.

23. Joe Hill, "The Preacher and the Slave," in IWW, *Songs of the Workers,* 9.

24. Ralph Rinzler, quoted in Wayne Erbson, *Rural Roots of Bluegrass: Songs, Stories, and History* (Pacific, MO: Native Ground, 2003), 118.

25. Guthrie, introduction to "I'm Goin' Down That Road Feeling Bad," *Hard Hitting Songs for Hard-Hit People,* ed. Alan Lomax, Woody Guthrie, and Pete Seeger (New York: Oak Publications, 1967), 215.

26. Guthrie, "Blowin' down the Road (I Ain't Going to Be Treated This Way)," on *Dust Bowl Ballads* (Buddha Records, 2000), track 6.

27. The Carter Family, "I'm Thinking Tonight of My Blue Eyes," on *The Carter Family: 1927–1934* (JSP Records, 2002), disc 1, track 22.

28. Guthrie, "Ain't Got a Cent," *Songs of Woody Guthrie,* ms. 17, Archive of Folk Culture, American Folklife Center, Library of Congress, AFC 1940/004 Woody Guthrie Manuscript Collection, box 1, folder 13.

29. The Carter Family, "I Can't Feel at Home in This World Anymore," on *The Carter Family: 1927–1934,* disc 3, track 17.

30. Guthrie, prefatory remarks to "I Ain't Got No Home," on *Library of Congress Recordings,* disc 2, track 5.

31. Guthrie, "I Ain't Got No Home," on *Hard Travelin': The Asch Recordings,* vol. 3, track 5.

32. Guthrie, annotation to manuscript lyrics to "Pretty Boy Floyd," in Woody Guthrie Archives, Tulsa, Oklahoma, Songs 1, box 2, folder 21.

33. Steinbeck, *Grapes of Wrath,* 38.

34. Guthrie, *Woody Sez* (New York: Grosset and Dunlap, 1975), 17.

35. Guthrie, "Notes on 'East Texas Red,'" Woody Guthrie Papers: Moses and Frances Asch Collection, Ralph Rinzler Archives, Center for Folklife and Cultural Heritage, Smithsonian Institution, Washington, DC, Song Texts, box 1, folder 3.

36. Guthrie, annotation to lyrics of "East Texas Red," Woody Guthrie Papers, Typescripts: Woody Guthrie Songs, box 2, folder 2.

37. See Arlo Guthrie, "East Texas Red," on Various Artists, *Folkways: A Vision Shared: A Tribute to Woody Guthrie and Leadbelly* (Columbia, 1988), track 7.

38. Guthrie, notes to "Hard Times in Cryderville Jail," in Lomax, Guthrie, and Seeger, *Hard Hitting Songs for Hard-Hit People*, 72.

39. Guthrie, introductory notes to Section IV: "And You Land in Jail," in Lomax, Guthrie, and Seeger, *Hard Hitting Songs for Hard-Hit People*, 67.

40. Denning, *Cultural Front*, 270.

41. Robert Sklar, *Movie-Made America: A Cultural History of American Movies* (New York: Random House, 1994), 181.

42. See Kevin Starr, *Endangered Dreams: The Great Depression in California* (New York: Oxford University Press, 1997), chapter 6.

43. Guthrie, "Jesse James and His Boys," in Lomax, Guthrie, and Seeger, *Hard Hitting Songs for Hard-Hit People*, 113.

44. Guthrie, notes to "Jesse James and His Boys," in Lomax, Guthrie, and Seeger, *Hard Hitting Songs for Hard-Hit People*, 112. For historical background to the Pinkerton attack, see Mark Lee Gardner, *Shot All to Hell: Jesse James, the Northfield Raid, and the Wild West's Greatest Escape* (New York: William Morrow, 2014), 48–50.

45. Mark Allan Jackson, *Prophet Singer: The Voice and Vision of Woody Guthrie* (Jackson: University Press of Mississippi, 2007), 168.

46. Guthrie, in Lomax, Guthrie, and Seeger, *Hard Hitting Songs for Hard-Hit People*, 18.

47. Guthrie, "Pretty Boy Floyd," on *Buffalo Skinners: The Asch Recordings*, vol. 4 (Smithsonian Folkways, 1999), track 5.

48. Unnamed *Sword of Truth* correspondent, quoted in Jim Bissett, *Agrarian Socialism in America* (Norman: University of Oklahoma Press, 1999), 88.

49. Guthrie, "Christ for President," as performed by Billy Bragg and Wilco on *Mermaid Avenue: The Complete Sessions* (Nonesuch, 2012), disc 1, track 9.

50. Guthrie, "They Laid Jesus Christ in His Grave," on *Library of Congress Recordings*, disc 2, track 3.

51. Guthrie, notes to "A Hard-Working Man Was Jesus," Woody Guthrie Archives, Tulsa, OK: Notebooks 1, notebook 4, p. 180.

52. Guthrie, "Vigilante Man," on *Dust Bowl Ballads*, track 12.

53. "John Hardy," in Alan Lomax, *Folksongs of North America* (Garden City, NY: Doubleday, 1960), 264.

54. Guthrie, "Tom Joad" (Part II), on *Dust Bowl Ballads*, track 8.

55. Guthrie, "Dust Bowl Refugee," on *Dust Bowl Ballads*, track 10.

56. Guthrie, *Bound for Glory*, 295.

CHAPTER 3

1. Peter La Chapelle, *Proud to Be an Okie: Cultural Politics, Country Music, and Migration to Southern California* (Berkeley: University of California Press, 2007), 49.

2. Guthrie, "Tom Joad" (Part I), *Dust Bowl Ballads* (Buddha Records, 2000), track 7.

3. Guthrie, "California, California," Woody Guthrie Archives, Tulsa, OK, Songs 1, box 1, folder 5.

4. Guthrie, "By the Valley So Green and the Ocean So Blue," *Songs of Woody Guthrie,* ms. 18, Archive of Folk Culture, American Folklife Center, Library of Congress, Washington, DC, AFC 1940/004 Woody Guthrie Manuscript Collection, box 1, folder 13.

5. Guthrie, quoted in Cray, *Ramblin' Man,* 95.

6. Guthrie, *Bound for Glory,* 294–95.

7. Guthrie, prefatory remarks to "Dust Bowl Refugee," on *Library of Congress Recordings* (Rounder, 1988), disc 3, track 6.

8. Worster, *Dust Bowl,* 52–53.

9. Buck Owens, quoted in Cray, *Ramblin' Man,* 134; La Chapelle, *Proud to Be an Okie,* 9.

10. La Chapelle, *Proud to Be an Okie,* 27–31.

11. H. L. Mencken, quoted in Worster, *Dust Bowl,* 53.

12. Gregory, *American Exodus,* 80.

13. Los Angeles mayor Frank L. Shaw, quoted in Martin Butler, *Voices of the Down and Out,* 136.

14. Guy Logsdon and Jeff Place, liner notes to Guthrie, *Buffalo Skinners: The Asch Recordings,* vol. 4 (Smithsonian Folkways, 1999), 24.

15. California Cavaliers official, quoted in Carey McWilliams, *Factories in the Field: The Story of Migratory Farm Labor in California* (Berkeley: University of California Press, 1999 [1939]), 240.

16. Guthrie, prefatory remarks to "Talking Dust Bowl Blues," on *Library of Congress Recordings,* disc 1, track 10.

17. Herman Cottrell, quoted in McWilliams, *Factories in the Field,* 240.

18. Guthrie, notes to "Vigilante Man," in Lomax, Guthrie, and Seeger, *Hard Hitting Songs for Hard-Hit People,* 234.

19. Guthrie, "Vigilante Man," on *Dust Bowl Ballads,* track 12.

20. Guthrie, "Old L.A.," as sung by Jay Farrar et al., *New Multitudes* (Rounder, 2012), disc 1, track 5.

21. Klein, *Woody Guthrie,* 92.

22. Guthrie, introduction to "Los Angeles New Years Flood," on *Library of Congress Recordings,* disc 3, track 8.

23. Guthrie, "Los Angeles New Years Flood," on *Library of Congress Recordings,* disc 3, track 8.

24. Guthrie, "I'm A-Goin' Back to the Farm," *Songs of Woody Guthrie,* ms. 203, Archive of Folk Culture, American Folklife Center, Library of Congress, AFC 1940/004 Woody Guthrie Manuscript Collection, box 1, folder 13.

25. Guthrie, *Woody Sez,* 56.

26. Guthrie, *Woody Sez,* 55.

27. Guthrie, prefatory remarks to "Dust Bowl Refugee," on *Library of Congress Recordings,* disc 3, track 5.

28. Guthrie, "Dust Bowl Refugee," on *Dust Bowl Ballads,* track 10.

29. Guthrie, notes to "Dust Bowl Refugee," in Lomax, Guthrie, and Seeger, *Hard Hitting Songs for Hard-Hit People,* 224.

30. La Chapelle, *Proud to Be an Okie,* 65.

31. Cray, *Ramblin' Man,* 170–71.

32. Cray, *Ramblin' Man,* 150.

33. Guthrie to Alan Lomax, September 19, 1940, Woody Guthrie Archives, Tulsa, OK, Correspondence Series 1, box 1, folder 39.

34. Denning, *Cultural Front,* 268.

35. Wayne Hampton, *Guerrilla Minstrels* (Knoxville: University of Tennessee Press, 1986), 105.

36. Guy Logsdon, Introduction to Guthrie, *Woody Sez,* xv.

37. Denning, *Cultural Front,* 260.

38. George Tupp, "You Okies and Arkies," quoted in Guthrie, "Arvin Migratory Labor Camp," no date, Woody Guthrie Archives, Manuscripts 2, box 1, folder 4.

39. Gregory, *American Exodus,* 154.

40. Guthrie, *Woody Sez,* 63–64.

41. Karl Marx and Friedrich Engels, *The Communist Manifesto* (New York: Monthly Review Press, 1964 [1848]), 94.

42. Guthrie, quoted in Jackson, *Prophet Singer,* 228–29.

43. Guthrie, in Lomax, Guthrie, and Seeger, *Hard Hitting Songs for Hard-Hit People,* 17.

44. See Robert Conquest, *The Harvest of Sorrow: Soviet Collectivization and the Terror-Famine* (Oxford: Oxford University Press, 1987).

45. Guthrie, notes to "Sharecropper Song," Woody Guthrie Papers: Moses and Frances Asch Collection, Ralph Rinzler Archives, Center for Folklife and Cultural Heritage, Smithsonian Institution, Washington, D, Song Texts, box 1, folder 7.

46. Guthrie, "More War News," quoted in Klein, *Woody Guthrie,* 135.

CHAPTER 4

1. Woody Guthrie, *Roll On, Columbia: The Columbia River Songs,* ed. Bill Murlin (Portland: Bonneville Power Administration, 1987), 49.

2. Elmer Buehler and Arlo Guthrie, quoted in *Roll On, Columbia: Woody Guthrie and the Bonneville Power Administration,* documentary produced and directed by Michael Majdic and Denise Edwards (University of Oregon, 2000).

3. Blaine Harden, *A River Lost: The Life and Death of the Columbia* (New York: Norton, 2012), 87.

4. Leonard Ortolano and Katherine Kao Cushing, *Grand Coulee Dam and the Columbia Basin Project, USA* (Cape Town: World Commission on Dams, 2000), v.

5. Klein, *Woody Guthrie,* 202.

6. Seeger, quoted in *Roll On, Columbia* (dir. Majdic and Edwards).

7. Hampton, *Guerrilla Minstrels*, 131.

8. Guthrie to Millard Lampell, no precise date (but May 1941), Woody Guthrie Archives, Correspondence Series 1, box 1, folder 34.

9. Cray, *Ramblin' Man*, 211.

10. Steven Kahn, quoted in Guthrie, *Roll On, Columbia*, 78.

11. Kahn, quoted in Cray, *Ramblin' Man*, 208–9, 211.

12. The twenty-one-minute film, along with other BPA propaganda films, is available for viewing on the BPA's YouTube channel: https://www.youtube.com /playlist?list=PLhze0rva6nVcLtUm9KnXTOH1-h7SFYgjc.

13. *The Columbia: America's Greatest Power Stream*, dir. Steven Kahn (US Department of the Interior, 1949).

14. *The Columbia*, dir. Kahn. This is also one of the few recorded versions of Guthrie playing this song in a minor key; the others are a restored BPA version on *Woody Guthrie: American Radical Patriot*, disc 5, track 2, and a live performance on *The Live Wire Woody Guthrie*, track 9.

15. *The Columbia*, dir. Kahn.

16. Meaning the B-17 bomber, nicknamed the "Flying Fortress."

17. *The Columbia*, dir. Kahn.

18. Guthrie, quoted in Cray, *Ramblin' Man*, 215.

19. Guthrie, quoted in Cray, *Ramblin' Man*, 215.

20. Bill Nowlin, companion text to *Woody Guthrie: American Radical Patriot* (Rounder, 2013), 131.

21. Guthrie, *Roll On, Columbia*, 3.

22. Official website, Washington Secretary of State: https://www.sos.wa.gov/seal /symbols_songs.aspx.

23. Ronald D. Cohen and Dave Samuelson, companion text to *Songs for Political Action: Folk Music, Topical Songs, and the American Left, 1926–1953* (Bear Family Records, 1996), 180.

24. Guthrie, "Roll On, Columbia," on *Woody Guthrie: American Radical Patriot* (Rounder, 2013), disc 5, track 4 (hereafter *WGARP*).

25. Nora Guthrie, quoted in *Roll On, Columbia*, dir. Majdic and Edwards.

26. Guthrie to Millard Lampell, no precise date, but May 1941, Woody Guthrie Archives, Correspondence Series 1, box 1, folder 34.

27. Guthrie, "Jackhammer Blues" ("Jackhammer John"), on *WGARP*, disc 5, track 13.

28. Guthrie, "Hard Travelin'," on *WGARP*, disc 5, track 11.

29. Guthrie, "Biggest Thing That Man Has Ever Done," on *WGARP*, disc 5, track 12.

30. Hampton, *Guerrilla Minstrels*, 133.

31. Guthrie to Lampell, May 1941, Woody Guthrie Archives, Correspondence Series 1, box 1, folder 34.

32. Guthrie, "Oregon Trail," on *WGARP*, disc 5, track 3.

33. Guthrie, "Columbia's Waters," on *WGARP*, disc 5, track 8.

34. Guthrie, "Washington Talkin' Blues," on *WGARP,* disc 5, track 16.

35. Guthrie, quoted in Cray, *Ramblin' Man,* 210.

36. Guthrie, "Talking Columbia," on *WGARP,* disc 5, track 6.

37. Guthrie, quoted in John Greenway, *American Folksongs of Protest* (New York: A. S. Barnes, 1953), 292.

38. Guthrie, "Talking Columbia," on *The Asch Recordings,* vol. 3: *Hard Travelin'* (Smithsonian Folkways, 1999), track 14.

39. Guthrie, "New Found Land," on *WGARP,* disc 5, track 5.

40. Guthrie, "Roll On, Columbia," on *WGARP,* disc 5, track 4.

41. Guthrie, "End of My Line," on *WGARP,* disc 5, track 19.

42. Guthrie, "Talking Columbia," on *WGARP,* disc 5, track 6.

43. Guthrie, "Roll, Columbia, Roll," on *WGARP,* disc 5, track 7.

44. Guthrie to Alan Lomax, February 15, 1941, Archive of Folk Culture, American Folklife Center, Library of Congress, Washington, DC, AFC 1940/004, Woody Guthrie Manuscript Collection, box 1, folder 3.

45. Guthrie, "Why Do You Stand There in the Rain," in Lomax, Guthrie, and Seeger, *Hard Hitting Songs for Hard-Hit People,* 363.

46. Guthrie, "Ramblin' Blues," on *WGARP,* disc 5, track 9.

47. Guthrie, "Grand Coulee Dam," on *WGARP,* disc 5, track 15.

48. Nowlin, companion text to *Woody Guthrie: American Radical Patriot,* 151.

49. Guthrie, "Columbia's Waters," in Guthrie, *Roll On, Columbia,* 43.

50. Guthrie, "Columbia's Waters," version on Woody Guthrie Publications website, http://woodyguthrie.org/Lyrics/Columbias_Waters.htm.

51. Guthrie, "Biggest Thing That Man Has Ever Done," on *WGARP,* disc 5, track 12.

52. Guthrie to Moses Asch, no precise date, but 1947, Woody Guthrie Archives, Correspondence Series 1, box 1, folder 8.

53. Stewart Udall, quoted in Hampton, *Guerrilla Minstrels,* 133.

54. Unnamed constituent to Senator Mark Hatfield, September 7, 1967. Woody Guthrie Archives, Woodrow W. Guthrie FBI Files, Personal Papers, box 2, folder 48.1.

CHAPTER 5

1. Klein, *Woody Guthrie,* 225.

2. Guthrie, "People's Songs and Its People," Woody Guthrie Archives, Manuscripts Series 1, box 4, folder 25.

3. Guthrie, "Voice," in Marsh and Leventhal, *Pastures of Plenty,* xxv.

4. Guthrie, "Biggest Thing That Man Has Ever Done," on *WGARP,* disc 5, track 12.

5. Guthrie to Marjorie Mazia, no precise date, but January 1943, Woody Guthrie Archives, Correspondence Series 1, box 1, folder 45.

6. The Almanac Singers, *Songs for John Doe* (Almanac Records, 1941).

7. Lee Hays, quoted in Doris Willins, *Lonesome Traveler: The Life of Lee Hays* (Lincoln: University of Nebraska Press, 1993), 69.

8. See Bill Nowlin, companion text to *Woody Guthrie: American Radical Patriot,* 209–20, for a detailed background to the sinking.

9. Guthrie and the Almanac Singers, "The Sinking of the Reuben James," on *WGARP,* disc 5, track 20.

10. Guthrie, "Lindbergh," on *This Land Is Your Land: The Asch Recordings,* vol. 1 (Smithsonian Folkways, 1999), track 6.

11. Guthrie, quoted in Denisoff, *Great Day Coming,* 91.

12. Guthrie, "Open Up That Second Front Today," Woody Guthrie Archives, Notebooks 1(3), p. 76.

13. Guthrie, "What Are We Waiting On?," on *Hard Travelin': The Asch Recordings,* vol. 3 (Smithsonian Folkways, 1999), track 18.

14. Guthrie, *Woody Sez,* 62.

15. Guthrie, "Ice in My Whiskers," Archive of Folk Culture, American Folklife Center, Library of Congress, Washington, DC, AFC 1940/004 Woody Guthrie Manuscript Collection, box 1, folder 15.

16. Guthrie, "You Fascists Bound to Lose," in *War Songs Are Work Songs,* typed ms., no page, in Alan Lomax Collection, American Folklife Center, Library of Congress, Washington, DC, AFC 2004/004, Woody Guthrie Manuscripts, box 33.02, folder 16.

17. The purported Yamamoto quote is in William Safire, *Safire's Political Dictionary* (New York: Oxford University Press, 2008), 666.

18. Guthrie, "Curly-Headed Baby," *War Songs Are Work Songs,* no page.

19. Guthrie, "Miss Pavilichenko," on *Hard Travelin': The Asch Recordings,* vol. 3, track 8.

20. Guthrie, "Let Me Join Your Army," Woody Guthrie Archives, Notebook 3, p. 68.

21. Guthrie, "So Long, It's Been Good to Know Yuh," Woody Guthrie Papers, Moses and Frances Asch Collection, Ralph Rinzler Archives, Center for Folklife and Cultural Heritage, Smithsonian Institution, Washington, DC, Song Texts, box 1, folder 7.

22. Guthrie, "War Bond Gal of Mine," *War Songs Are Work Songs,* no page.

23. Guy Logsdon and Jeff Place, liner notes to Guthrie, *Buffalo Skinners: The Asch Recordings,* vol. 4 (Smithsonian Folkways, 1999), 12.

24. Guthrie, "Ranger's Command," on *Buffalo Skinners: The Asch Recordings,* vol. 4, track 1.

25. Guthrie to Marjorie Mazia, January 25, 1943, Woody Guthrie Archives, Correspondence Series 1, box 1, folder 45.

26. Guthrie, "Seamen Three," in Marsh and Leventhal, *Pastures of Plenty,* 135.

27. Cisco Houston, quoted in Jim Longhi, *Woody, Cisco, and Me: With Woody Guthrie in the Merchant Marine* (New York: ibooks, 2004), 46.

28. Guthrie, "Talking Sailor," on *Hard Travelin': The Asch Recordings,* vol. 3, track 17, and Ramblin' Jack Elliott, *Talking Woody Guthrie* (Topic, 1963), side 2, track 5.

29. Guthrie, "Talking Sailor," on *Hard Travelin'.*

30. Guthrie, "When My Good Ship Went Down," Woody Guthrie Archives, Lyrics Series 1, box 9.

31. Guthrie, "Sicily Will Rise from Its Ruins," in Marsh and Leventhal, *Pastures of Plenty,* 136.

32. Guthrie, "Sicily Will Rise from Its Ruins," in Marsh and Leventhal, *Pastures of Plenty,* 134–35.

33. Longhi, *Woody, Cisco, and Me,* 169–70.

34. Guthrie, "The Rubaiyat," on *Hard Travelin',* track 25.

35. David Amram, "Ringing the Bells of Freedom in 1950s East Village," *New York Times,* January 23, 2012, http://eastvillage.thelocal.nytimes.com/2012/01/23/david-amram-ringing-the-bells-of-freedom-in-1950s-east-village/.

36. Guthrie, notes to "London City," in *New Found Land,* typed ms., no page, Alan Lomax Collection, American Folklife Center, Library of Congress, Washington, DC, AFC 2004/004, Woody Guthrie Manuscripts, box 33.02, folder 20.

37. Guthrie, "London City," Woody Guthrie Archives, Notebook 77, p. 98.

38. Klein, *Woody Guthrie,* 280.

39. Guthrie, "Better World A-Comin'," on *Hard Travelin',* Track 7.

40. Guthrie, "Keep That Oil A-Rollin'," on *Songs for Political Action* (Bear Family Records, 1996), disc 4, track 8.

41. Guthrie, quoted in Klein, *Woody Guthrie,* 331.

42. Guthrie to Marjorie Mazia, June 11, 1944, Woody Guthrie Archives, Correspondence Series 1, box 1, folder 50.

43. Guthrie, "Union's My Religion," quoted in Klein, *Woody Guthrie,* 281.

44. Guthrie, "Union Labor or Slave Labor," Woody Guthrie Archives, Manuscripts 1, box 4, folder 16.

45. Guthrie, "Peoples Songs and Its People," Woody Guthrie Archives, Manuscripts 1, box 4, folder 25.

46. Guthrie, "When I Get Home," as sung by Jay Farrar et al., on *New Multitudes* (Rounder, 2012), disc 2, track 9.

47. Guthrie, quoted in Klein, *Woody Guthrie,* 309.

48. Guthrie, quoted in Cray, *Ramblin' Man,* 305.

49. Guthrie to Moses Asch, July 15, 1946, Woody Guthrie Archives, Correspondence Series 1, box 1, folder 6.

50. Guthrie, "World's on Fire," as sung by Jay Farrar et al., on *New Multitudes,* disc 2, track 8.

51. Guthrie, "Post War Breakout," as sung by Anti-Flag, on *The Terror State* (Fat Wreck Chords, 2003), track 3.

52. Guthrie to the Almanac Singers, no date, but 1941, Woody Guthrie Archives, Correspondence Series 1, box 1, folder 3.

CHAPTER 6

1. Steven Brower and Nora Guthrie, eds., *Woody Guthrie Artworks* (New York: Rizzoli, 2005).

2. Guthrie to the Almanac Singers, March 18, 1941, Woody Guthrie Archives, Correspondence Series 1, box 1, folder 3.

3. Guthrie, *Woody Sez*, 116.

4. Guthrie, *Woody Sez*, 105–6.

5. Guthrie, *Woody Sez*, 106.

6. Will Geer, quoted in Cray, *Ramblin' Man*, 172.

7. Guthrie to the Almanac Singers, no date, but 1941, Woody Guthrie Archives, Correspondence Series 1, box 1, folder 3.

8. Guthrie, "I Don't Feel at Home on the Bowery No More," in Nora Guthrie and Woody Guthrie Archives, *My Name Is New York: Ramblin' around Woody Guthrie's Town* (Brooklyn, NY: powerHouse Books, 2012), 15.

9. Guthrie, "Manifesto on Wage Slaves, Sleep Walking, and Jesus," ms. 1, Alan Lomax Collection, American Folklife Center, Library of Congress, Washington, DC, AFC 2004/04, box 33.03, folder 03.

10. Guthrie, "The New York Trains," in *My Name Is New York*, 28.

11. Guthrie, "Talkin' Subway Blues," in *My Name Is New York*, 25.

12. Guthrie, "New York Town," on *This Land Is Your Land: The Asch Recordings*, vol. 1 (Smithsonian Folkways, 1999), track 11.

13. Guthrie, notes to "Jesus Christ," companion text to *The Live Wire Woody Guthrie*, 51.

14. Guthrie, introduction to "Jesus Christ Was a Man," in Lomax, Guthrie, and Seeger, *Hard Hitting Songs for Hard-Hit People*, 336.

15. Guthrie, "Jesus Christ," on *This Land Is Your Land: The Asch Recordings*, vol. 1, track 13.

16. Nora Guthrie, on *My Name Is New York* (Woody Guthrie Publications, 2014), disc 1, track 2.

17. Alan Lomax, quoted in Denisoff, *Great Day Coming*, 73.

18. Hampton, *Guerrilla Minstrels*, 108.

19. Guthrie, "How to Make Up a Balladsong and Get Away with It," in Marsh and Leventhal, *Pastures of Plenty*, 71.

20. Sender Garlin, quoted in Cray, *Ramblin' Man*, 171.

21. Mike Quin, quoted in Denisoff, *Great Day Coming*, 68.

22. Saul Bellow, quoted in Klein, *Woody Guthrie*, 162.

23. Irwin Silber, quoted in Cray, *Ramblin' Man*, 216, 294.

24. Denisoff, *Great Day Coming*, 69.

25. Lampell, quoted in Lieberman, *"My Song Is My Weapon,"* 53, 62.

26. Guthrie to Lomax, September 19, 1940, Woody Guthrie Archives, Correspondence Series 1, box 1, folder 39.

27. Guthrie to Lomax, September 19, 1940, Woody Guthrie Archives, Correspondence Series 1, box 1, folder 39.

28. Guthrie, "Union Air in Union Square," in Marsh and Leventhal, *Pastures of Plenty,* 123–24.

29. Guthrie, "Mermaid's Avenue," as sung by the Klezmatics, on *Wonder Wheel* (Jewish Music Group, 2006), track 2.

30. Guthrie, "Go Coney Island, Roll on the Sand," as sung by the Demolition String Band and Stephan Said on *My Name Is New York,* disc 3, track 13.

31. Guthrie to Will and Herta Geer, November 12, 1944, Woody Guthrie Archives, Correspondence Series 1, box 1, folder 18.

32. Guthrie, "To a Union Show Troup," Woody Guthrie Archives, Manuscripts, box 1, folder 12.

33. Guthrie, "The Bowery and Me," in Marsh and Leventhal, *Pastures of Plenty,* 190–91.

34. Seeger, quoted in Lieberman, *"My Song Is My Weapon,"* 62.

35. Denisoff, *Great Day Coming,* 103.

36. Guthrie, "People's Songs and Its People," Woody Guthrie Archives, Manuscripts, box 4, folder 25.

37. Bryan K. Garman, *A Race of Singers: Whitman's Working-Class Hero from Guthrie to Springsteen* (Chapel Hill: University of North Carolina Press, 2000), 142.

38. Guthrie, "Ninety Mile Wind," as sung by Hans-Eckardt Wenzel on *Ticky Tock: Wenzel Sings Woody Guthrie* (Contraer Musik, 2003), track 13.

39. Guthrie, "Voice," as sung by Ani DiFranco on Rob Wasserman and Friends, *The Note of Hope* (429 Records, 2011), track 7.

40. Guthrie, "My Name Is New York," in *My Name Is New York,* 10.

CHAPTER 7

1. "Beluthahatchee," Florida Department of State, Division of Historical Resources, Florida Historical Markers Programs, http://apps.flheritage.com/markers/markers.cfm?ID=st.%20johns.

2. Jorge Arévalo Mateus, "Beluthahatchee Blues: An Interview with Stetson Kennedy," in Chris Green et al., eds., *Radicalism in the South Since Reconstruction* (New York: Palgrave Macmillan, 2006), 213.

3. Guthrie, narration to "Lost Train Blues," on *Library of Congress Recordings* (Rounder, 1988), disc 1, track 1.

4. Guthrie, "How Much, How Long," on *The Live Wire Woody Guthrie*, track 1.

5. Klein, *Woody Guthrie,* 95–96.

6. La Chapelle, *Proud to Be an Okie,* 66.

7. Guthrie, notes to "Don't Lie to Me," *Ten of Woody Guthrie's Songs: Book One,* typed manuscript, 5, Archive of Folk Culture, American Folklife Center, Library of Congress, Washington, DC, AFC 1940/004, Woody Guthrie Manuscript Collection, box 1, folder 14.

8. Guthrie, "Southern White Wombanhood," Woody Guthrie Archives (hereafter WGA), Notebooks 2(11) (no date), 59.

9. Guthrie, "Big North Sea," WGA, Notebooks 2(11), 89. June 1953.

10. WGA, Notebooks 2(11), 91.

11. WGA, Notebooks 2(11) (no date), 92.

12. WGA, Notebooks 2(11) (no date), 88.

13. WGA, Notebooks 2(11) (no date), 86.

14. WGA, Notebooks 2(11) (no date), 94.

15. Will Kaufman, "Woody Guthrie, 'Old Man Trump,' and a Real Estate Empire's Racist Foundations," *The Conversation,* January 21, 2016, https://theconversation.com/woody-guthrie-old-man-trump-and-a-real-estate-empires-racist-foundations-53026.

16. Guthrie, "Black Feet," WGA, Notebooks 1(57), 91. August 16, 1947.

17. Guthrie to Marjorie Mazia, no precise date, but January 1943, Woody Guthrie Archives, Correspondence Series 1, box 1, folder 45.

18. Guthrie, "Racial Hate at Beach Haven," WGA, Notebooks 2(9), 107. February 26, 1952.

19. Guthrie, "Beach Haven Race Hate," WGA, Notebooks 2(2), 73. 1954.

20. Guthrie, "Sweety Black Girl," WGA, Notebooks 2(6), p. 31. October 19, 1950.

21. Arévalo Mateus, "Beluthahatchee Blues," 212.

22. Guthrie to Stetson Kennedy, August 15, 1950, WGA, Correspondence Series 1, box 1, folder 32.

23. WGA, Notebooks 2(1), 1. April 1953.

24. Kennedy, "The Klan Unmasked," http://www.stetsonkennedy.com/klan.htm.

25. Kennedy, "Palmetto Country," http://www.stetsonkennedy.com/palmetto.htm.

26. Guthrie to Stetson Kennedy, undated. The letter is reprinted in the Woody Guthrie Archives online guide to the Stetson Kennedy Papers: http://woodyguthriecenter.org/archives/collection/guide-to-the-stetson-kennedy-papers/.

27. Stetson Kennedy, *The Jim Crow Guide: The Way It Was* (Boca Raton: University Press of Florida, 1990), 161.

28. Diane Roberts, "The Ballad of Stetson Kennedy," *St. Petersburg Times,* March 7, 2004, http://www.sptimes.com/2004/03/07/news_pf/Perspective/The_Ballad_of_Stetson.shtml.

29. Guthrie, "Stetson Kennedy," as sung by Billy Bragg and Wilco, on *Mermaid Avenue: The Complete Sessions* (Nonesuch, 2012), disc 2, track 7.

30. Cray, *Ramblin' Man,* 342–43.

31. Klein, *Woody Guthrie,* 383.

32. Gary Mormino, quoted in Paul Ortiz, "Voices: Stetson Kennedy and the Pursuit of Truth," Institute for Southern Studies, *Facing South,* August 30, 2011, http://www.southernstudies.org/2011/08/voices-stetson-kennedy-and-the-pursuit-of-truth.html.

33. Guthrie, "Beluthahatchee Bill," reprinted in Stetson Kennedy, *The Klan Unmasked* (Tuscaloosa: University of Alabama Press, 2011), 271.

34. Kennedy, *Jim Crow Guide,* 8. All other page numbers are referenced parenthetically.

35. Guthrie, "Pineytimber Blues," WGA, Notebooks 2(11) (no date), 93.

36. Kennedy in Arévalo Mateus, "Beluthahatchee Blues," 217.

37. Guthrie, "Ellis Island Outlaw," WGA, Notebooks 2(3) (no date), 37.

38. Guthrie, "Narrow Margin," WGA, Notebooks 2(3) (no date), 92.

39. Guthrie, "Pistol Packer," WGA, Notebooks 2(3) (no date), 94.

40. Guthrie to Moses Asch, August 26, 1953, WGA, Correspondence Series 1, box 1, folder 9.

41. Guthrie, "Get Rid of That," WGA, Notebooks 2(4) (no date), 87.

CONCLUSION

1. Guthrie, "Einstein Theme Song," in Shelton, *Born to Win*, 192.

2. Guthrie, "Einstein Theme Song," in Shelton, *Born to Win*, 192–93.

3. Guthrie, "Another Man's Done Gone," as sung by Billy Bragg and Wilco on *Mermaid Avenue: The Complete Sessions* (Nonesuch, 2012), disc 1, track 14.

4. Guthrie, notes to "Dream of a Miner's Child," Woody Guthrie Archives (WGA), Songs 1, box 2.

5. Guthrie, notes to "Go Left and Be Right," WGA, Songs 1, box 3.

6. Guthrie, notes to "It Was Down in Old Pearl Harbor," WGA, Songs 1, box 4.

7. Guthrie, quoted in Cray, *Ramblin' Man*, 343.

8. Guy Logsdon and Jeff Place, liner notes to Guthrie, *The Asch Recordings,* Vol. 1: *This Land Is Your Land*.

9. Butler, *Voices of the Down and Out,* 58.

10. Guthrie, "People I Owe," in Shelton, *Born to Win,* 18.

SOURCES

PRINTED AND ONLINE

Allred, Jeff. *American Modernism and Depression Documentary.* New York: Oxford University Press, 2009.

Amram, David. "Ringing the Bells of Freedom in 1950s East Village." *New York Times,* January 23, 2012.

Arévalo Mateus, Jorge. "Beluthahatchee Blues: An Interview with Stetson Kennedy." In *Radicalism in the South since Reconstruction,* edited by Chris Green, Rachel Rubin, and James Smethurst, 211–26. New York: Palgrave Macmillan, 2006.

"Beluthahatchee." *Florida Historical Markers Programs.* Florida Department of State, Division of Historical Resources. http://apps.flheritage.com/markers/markers.cfm?ID=st.%20johns.

Bennett, Sanford F., and Joseph P. Webster. "In the Sweet By and By." In *Evening Light Songs.* Guthrie, OK: Faith Publishing House, 1949.

Bissett, Jim. *Agrarian Socialism in America.* Norman: University of Oklahoma Press, 1999.

Brower, Steven, and Nora Guthrie. *Woody Guthrie Artworks.* New York: Rizzoli, 2005.

Buehler, Phillip, ed. *Woody Guthrie's Wardy Forty: The Interviews.* Mt. Kisco, NY: Woody Guthrie Publications, 2013.

Buehler, Phillip, with Nora Guthrie and the Woody Guthrie Archives. *Woody Guthrie's Wardy Forty: Greystone Park State Hospital Revisited.* Mt. Kisco, NY: Woody Guthrie Publications, 2013.

Burbank, Garin. *When Farmers Voted Red: The Gospel of Socialism in the Oklahoma Countryside, 1910–1924.* Westport, CT: Greenwood Press, 1976.

Butler, Martin. *Voices of the Down and Out: The Dust Bowl Migration and the Great Depression in the Songs of Woody Guthrie.* Heidelberg, Germany: Universitätsverlag Winter, 2007.

Camus, Albert. "The Myth of Sisyphus." In *The Myth of Sisyphus and Other Essays,* translated by Justin O'Brien, 119–23. New York: Vintage, 1991.

Cantor, Milton. *The Divided Left: American Radicalism, 1900–1975.* New York: Hill and Wang, 1978.

Cantwell, Robert. *When We Were Good: The Folk Revival.* Cambridge, MA: Harvard University Press, 1996.

Carpenter, Damian A. *Lead Belly, Woody Guthrie, Bob Dylan, and American Folk Outlaw Performance.* Abingdon: Routledge, 2018.

Cohen, Ronald D. *Folk Music: The Basics.* London: Routledge, 2006.

———. *Woody Guthrie: Writing America's Songs.* New York: Routledge, 2012.

———. *Work and Sing: A History of Occupational and Labor Union Songs in the United States.* Crockett, CA: Carquinez Press, 2010.

Cohen, Ronald D., and Dave Samuelson. *Songs for Political Action: Folk Music, Topical Songs and the American Left, 1926–1953.* Hambergen, Germany: Bear Family Records, 1996.

Comentale, Edward P. *Sweet Air: Modernism, Regionalism, and American Popular Song.* Urbana: University of Illinois Press, 2013.

Conquest, Robert. *The Harvest of Sorrow: Soviet Collectivization and the Terror-Famine.* Oxford: Oxford University Press, 1987.

Cray, Ed. *Ramblin' Man: The Life and Times of Woody Guthrie.* New York: W. W. Norton, 2004.

Cunningham, Agnes "Sis," and Gordon Friesen. *Red Dust and Broadsides: A Joint Biography,* edited by Ronald D. Cohen. Amherst: University of Massachusetts Press, 1999.

Denisoff, R. Serge. *Great Day Coming: Folk Music and the American Left.* Baltimore: Penguin, 1973.

Denning, Michael. *The Cultural Front: The Laboring of American Culture in the Twentieth Century.* London: Verso, 1998.

Dunaway, David King. *How Can I Keep from Singing? The Ballad of Pete Seeger.* New York: Villard Books, 2008.

Dunaway, David King, and Molly Beer, eds. *Singing Out: An Oral History of America's Folk Music Revivals.* New York: Oxford University Press, 2010.

Duncan, Dayton, and Ken Burns. *The Dust Bowl: An Illustrated History.* San Francisco: Chronicle Books, 2012.

Edgmon, Mary Jo Guthrie, and Guy Logsdon. *Woody's Road: Woody Guthrie's Letters Home, Drawings, Photos, and Other Unburied Treasures.* Boulder, CO: Paradigm, 2012.

Erbsen, Wayne. *Rural Roots of Bluegrass: Songs, Stories and History.* Pacific, MO: Native Ground Music, 2003.

Foley, Hugh W., Jr. *Oklahoma Music Guide II.* Stillwater, OK: New Forums Press, 2014.

Garman, Bryan K. *A Race of Singers: Whitman's Working-Class Hero from Guthrie to Springsteen.* Chapel Hill: University of North Carolina Press, 2000.

Goldsmith, Peter D. *Making People's Music: Moe Asch and Folkways Records* (Washington, DC: Smithsonian Institution Press, 1998.

Graff, Ellen. *Stepping Left: Dance and Politics in New York City, 1928–1942.* Durham, NC: Duke University Press, 1997.

Green, Archie, et al., eds. *The Big Red Songbook.* Chicago: Charles H. Kerr Publishing, 2007.

Gregory, James N. *American Exodus: The Dust Bowl Migration and Okie Culture in California*. Oxford: Oxford University Press, 1989.

Greenway, John. *American Folksongs of Protest*. New York: A. S. Barnes, 1953.

Guthrie, Nora, and Woody Guthrie Archives. *My Name Is New York: Ramblin' around Woody Guthrie's Town*. Brooklyn, NY: powerHouse Books, 2012.

Guthrie, Woody. *American Folksong*, edited by Moses Asch. New York: Oak Publications, 1961.

———. *Born to Win*, edited by Robert Shelton. New York: Collier Books, 1967.

———. *Bound for Glory*. New York: E. P. Dutton, 1943.

———. *House of Earth: A Novel*, edited by Douglas Brinkley and Johnny Depp. New York: HarperCollins/Infinitum Nihil, 2013.

———. *Pastures of Plenty*, edited by Dave Marsh and Harold Leventhal. New York: HarperPerennial, 1990.

———. *Roll On, Columbia: The Columbia River Songs*, edited by Bill Murlin. Portland, OR: Bonneville Power Administration, 1988.

———. *Seeds of Man: An Experience Lived and Dreamed*. New York: Pocket Books, 1977.

———. *Woody Guthrie Folk Songs*. New York: Ludlow Music, 1963.

———. *Woody Guthrie Song Book*, edited by Harold Leventhal and Marjorie Guthrie. New York: Grosset and Dunlap, 1976.

———. *Woody Sez*, edited by Marjorie Guthrie et al. New York Grosset and Dunlap, 1975.

Hampton, Wayne. *Guerrilla Minstrels*. Knoxville: University of Tennessee Press, 1986.

Harden, Blaine. *A River Lost: The Life and Death of the Columbia*. New York: W. W. Norton, 2012.

Harrington, Michael. *The Other America: Poverty in the United States*. New York: Touchstone, 1997.

Hawes, Bess Lomax. *Sing It Pretty: A Memoir*. Urbana: University of Illinois Press, 2008.

Hays, Lee. *Sing Out, Warning! Sing Out, Love! The Writings of Lee Hays*, edited by Robert S. Koppelman. Amherst: University of Massachusetts Press, 2004.

Henderson, Caroline. *Letters from the Dust Bowl*, edited by Alvin O. Turner. Norman: University of Oklahoma Press, 2001.

Hernandez, Tim Z. *All They Will Call You*. Tucson: University of Arizona Press, 2017.

Herzen, Alexander I. "A Letter Criticizing *The Bell*." In *A Herzen Reader*, edited and translated by Kathleen Parthé. Evanston, IL: Northwestern University Press, 2012.

Holter, Darryl, and William Deverell. *Woody Guthrie L.A.: 1937–1941*. Santa Monica, CA: Angel City Press, 2015.

Industrial Workers of the World. *Songs of the Workers to Fan the Flames of Discontent*. Chicago: IWW Publishing Bureau, 1964.

Isserman, Maurice. *Which Side Were You On? The American Communist Party during the Second World War.* Champaign: University of Illinois Press, 1993.

Jackson, Mark Allan. *Prophet Singer: The Voice and Vision of Woody Guthrie.* Jackson: University Press of Mississippi, 2007.

Kaufman, Will. "In Another Newly Discovered Song, Woody Guthrie Continues His Assault on 'Old Man Trump.'" *The Conversation,* September 6, 2016. https://theconversation.com/in-another-newly-discovered-song-woody-guthrie-continues-his-assault-on-old-man-trump-64221.

———. *Woody Guthrie, American Radical.* Urbana: University of Illinois Press, 2011.

———. "Woody Guthrie, 'Old Man Trump,' and a Real Estate Empire's Racist Foundations." *The Conversation,* January 21, 2016. https://theconversation.com/woody-guthrie-old-man-trump-and-a-real-estate-empires-racist-foundations-53026.

———. *Woody Guthrie's Modern World Blues.* Norman: University of Oklahoma Press, 2017.

———. "Woody Guthrie's 'Songs Against Franco.'" *Atlantis* 39, no. 1 (2017). https://www.atlantisjournal.org/index.php?journal=atlantis&page=article&op=view&path%5B%5D=349.

Kennedy, Stetson. *The Klan Unmasked.* Tuscaloosa: University of Alabama Press, 2011.

———. *The Jim Crow Guide: The Way It Was.* Boca Raton: University Press of Florida, 1990.

Klein, Joe. *Woody Guthrie: A Life.* New York: Delta, 1999.

La Chapelle, Peter. *Proud to Be an Okie: Cultural Politics, Country Music, and Migration to Southern California.* Berkeley: University of California Press, 2007.

Library of Congress. *New Deal Programs: Selected Library of Congress Resources.* Washington, DC: Library of Congress. http://www.loc.gov/rr/program/bib/newdeal/afc.html.

Lieberman, Robbie. *"My Song Is My Weapon": People's Songs, American Communism, and the Politics of Culture, 1930–1950.* Urbana: University of Illinois Press, 1995.

Lomax, Alan, ed. *Folksongs of North America.* Garden City, NY: Smithmark, 1960.

Lomax, Alan, Woody Guthrie, and Pete Seeger, eds. *Hard Hitting Songs for Hard-Hit People.* New York: Oak Publications, 1967.

Longhi, Jim. *Woody, Cisco and Me: With Woody Guthrie in the Merchant Marine.* New York: ibooks, 2004.

Marx, Karl, and Freidrich Engels. *The Communist Manifesto.* New York: Monthly Review Press, 1964. First published 1848.

McWilliams, Carey. *Factories in the Field: The Story of Migratory Farm Labor in California.* Berkeley: University of California Press, 2000.

Nowlin, Bill. *Woody Guthrie: Radical American Patriot.* Cambridge, MA: Rounder Records, 2013.

Ortiz, Paul. "Voices: Stetson Kennedy and the Pursuit of Truth." Institute for

Southern Studies: *Facing South,* August 30, 2011. http://www.southernstudies
.org/2011/08/voices-stetson-kennedy-and-the-pursuit-of-truth.html.

Ortolano, Leonard, and Katherine Kao Cushing. *Grand Coulee Dam and the Columbia Basin Project, USA.* Cape Town, South Africa: World Commission on Dams, 2000.

Overduin, James. "Einstein's Spacetime." In *Gravity Probe B: Testing Einstein's Universe.* Stanford University, 2007. https://einstein.stanford.edu/SPACETIME /spacetime2.html.

Partridge, Elizabeth. *This Land Was Made for You and Me: The Life and Songs of Woody Guthrie.* New York: Viking Press, 2002.

Partington, John S., ed. *The Life, Music, and Thought of Woody Guthrie.* Farnham, UK: Ashgate Publishers, 2011.

Reuss, Richard A., with JoAnne C. Reuss. *American Folk Music and Left-Wing Politics, 1927–1957.* London: Scarecrow Press, 2000.

Robbin, Ed. *Woody Guthrie and Me.* Berkeley, CA: Lancaster-Miller, 1979.

Roberts, Diane. "The Ballad of Stetson Kennedy." *St. Petersburg Times,* March 7, 2004.

Russell, Tony. *Country Music Originals: The Legends and the Lost.* New York: Oxford University Press, 2010.

Safire, William. *Safire's Political Dictionary.* New York: Oxford University Press, 2008.

Santelli, Robert. *This Land Is Your Land: Woody Guthrie and the Journey of an American Song.* Philadelphia: Running Press, 2012.

Santelli, Robert, and Emily Davidson, eds. *Hard Travelin': The Life and Legacy of Woody Guthrie.* Hanover, NH: Wesleyan University Press, 1999.

Shaw, John. *This Land That I Love: Irving Berlin, Woody Guthrie, and the Story of Two American Anthems.* New York: Public Affairs, 2013.

Sklar, Robert. *Movie-Made America: A Cultural History of American Movies.* New York: Vintage, 1994.

Smith, Gibbs M. *Joe Hill.* Layton, UT: Gibbs M. Smith, 1969.

Standish, David. "*Playboy* Interview." In *Conversations with Kurt Vonnegut,* edited by William Rodney Allen, 76–110. Jackson: University Press of Mississippi, 1999.

Starr, Kevin. *Endangered Dreams: The Great Depression in California.* New York: Oxford University Press, 1997.

Steinbeck, John. *The Grapes of Wrath.* London: Penguin, 2006. First published 1939.

Stott, William. *Documentary Expression and Thirties America.* Chicago: University of Chicago Press, 1986.

United States House of Representatives. *Investigation of Un-American Propaganda Activities in the United States.* Washington, DC: US Government Publishing Office, 1941.

Vandy, Greg, and Daniel Person. *26 Songs in 30 Days: Woody Guthrie's Columbia River Songs and the Planned Promised Land in the Pacific Northwest.* Seattle: Sasquatch Books, 2016.

Washington Secretary of State. *State Songs.* https://www.sos.wa.gov/seal/symbols _songs.aspx.

Weissman, Dick. *Which Side Are You On? An Inside History of the Folk Music Revival in America.* London: Continuum, 2006.

Whitman, Walt. *Complete Poetry and Collected Prose,* ed. Justin Kaplan. New York: Literary Classics of the United States, 1982.

Willens, Doris. *Lonesome Traveler: The Life of Lee Hays.* Lincoln: University of Nebraska Press, 1993.

Wolff, Daniel. *Grown-Up Anger: The Connected Mysteries of Bob Dylan, Woody Guthrie, and the Calumet Massacre of 1913.* New York: HarperCollins, 2017.

Worster, Donald. *Dust Bowl: The Southern Plains in the 1930s.* New York: Oxford University Press, 1982.

Yurchenko, Henrietta. *A Mighty Hard Road: The Woody Guthrie Story.* New York: McGraw-Hill, 1970.

Zieger, Robert H. *The CIO, 1935–1955.* Chapel Hill: University of North Carolina Press, 1997.

AUDIO

Almanac Singers. *Deep Sea Shanties.* General Records, 1941.

———. *Sod Buster Ballads.* General Records, 1941.

———. *Songs for John Doe.* Almanac Records, 1941.

Amram, David, and the Colorado Symphony Orchestra. *This Land: Symphonic Variations on a Song by Woody Guthrie.* Newport Classics Recordings, 2015.

Anti-Flag. *The Terror State.* Fat Wreck Chords, 2003.

Bragg, Billy, and Wilco. *Mermaid Avenue: The Complete Sessions.* Nonesuch, 2012.

Brooke, Jonatha. *The Works.* Bad Dog Records, 2008.

Carter Family. *The Carter Family: 1927–1934.* JSP Records, 2002.

Del McCoury Band. *Del and Woody.* McCoury Music, 2016.

Farrar, Jay, et al. *New Multitudes.* Rounder, 2012.

Guthrie, Arlo, with the Dillards. *32 Cents/Postage Due.* Rising Son Records, 2008.

Guthrie, Arlo, and the Guthrie Family. *20 Grow Big Songs.* Rising Son International, 1992.

Guthrie, Arlo, and Wenzel. *Every 100 Years.* Indigo Musik, 2010.

Guthrie, Nora, and Woody Guthrie Archives. *My Name Is New York Audio Book.* Woody Guthrie Publications, 2014.

Guthrie, Woody. *The Asch Recordings,* 4 vols. Smithsonian Folkways, 1999. Vol. 1, *This Land Is Your Land;* Vol. 2, *Muleskinner Blues;* Vol. 3, *Hard Travelin';* Vol. 4, *Buffalo Skinners.*

———. *Ballads of Sacco and Vanzetti.* Smithsonian Folkways, 1996.

———. *The Columbia River Collection.* Rounder, 1987.

———. *Dust Bowl Ballads.* Buddha Records, 2000.

———. *Library of Congress Recordings.* Rounder, 1988.

———. *The Live Wire Woody Guthrie.* Woody Guthrie Foundation, 2007.

———. *Long Ways to Travel: The Unreleased Folkways Masters, 1944–1949*. Smithsonian Folkways, 1994.

———. *The Martins and the Coys: The Alan Lomax Collection*. Rounder, 2000.

———. *My Dusty Road*. Rounder, 2009.

———. *Nursery Days*. Smithsonian Folkways, 1992.

———. *Songs to Grow On for Mother and Child*. Smithsonian Folkways, 1991.

———. *Struggle*. Smithsonian Folkways, 1990.

———. *Woody at 100: The Woody Guthrie Centennial Collection*. Smithsonian Folkways, 2012.

———. *Woody Guthrie: American Radical Patriot*. Rounder, 2013.

———. *Woody Guthrie Sings Folk Songs*. Smithsonian Folkways, 1992.

Harvey, Ryan, with Tom Morello and Ani DiFranco. "Old Man Trump." Firebrand Records, 2016.

Holter, Darryl. *Radio Songs: Woody Guthrie in Los Angeles, 1937–1939*. CD Baby, 2015.

Klezmatics. *Wonder Wheel*. Jewish Music Group, 2009.

———. *Woody Guthrie's Happy Joyous Hanukkah*. Jewish Music Group, 2006.

McDonald, Country Joe. *Thinking of Woody Guthrie*. Vanguard, 1969.

———. *A Tribute to Woody Guthrie*. Rag Baby Records, 2008.

Rafael, Joel. *The Songs of Woody Guthrie*. Inside Recordings, 2009.

Various artists. *Daddy-O Daddy*. Rounder, 2001.

———. *Ribbon of Highway, Endless Skyway*. Music Road Records, 2008.

———. *Roll Columbia: Woody Guthrie's 26 Northwest Songs*. Smithsonian Folkways, 2017.

———. *Songs for Political Action: Folk Music, Topical Songs, and the American Left, 1926–1953*. Bear Family Records, 1996.

———. *That's Why We're Marching: World War II and the American Folk Song Movement*. Smithsonian Folkways, 1996.

———. *Til We Outnumber 'Em: The Songs of Woody Guthrie*. Righteous Babe, 2000.

———. *A Vision Shared: A Tribute to Woody Guthrie and Lead Belly*. Columbia, 1988.

———. *Woody Guthrie: Hard Travelin'*. Rising Son Records, 2000.

———. *Woody Guthrie: The Tribute Concerts*. Bear Family Records, 2017.

———. *Woody at 100! Live at the Kennedy Center*. Sony Legacy, 2013.

Wasserman, Rob, and Friends. *Note of Hope*. 429 Records, 2011.

Wenzel, Hans-Eckardt. *Ticky Tock*. Contraer Musik, 2003.

VIDEO

Ashby, Hal, director. *Bound for Glory*. United Artists, 1976.

Frumkin, Peter, director. *Woody Guthrie: Ain't Got No Home*. PBS/American Masters, 2007.

Gammond, Stephen, director. *Woody Guthrie: This Machine Kills Fascists*. Snapper Music, 2005.

Haynes, Todd, director. *I'm Not There.* Endgame/Killer/Goldwyn/Wells, 2007.

Kahn, Steven, director. *The Columbia: America's Greatest Power Stream.* Bonneville Power Administration, 1949.

Lee, Paul, director. *Arena: Woody Guthrie.* British Broadcasting Corporation, 1988.

Majdic, Michael, and Denise Edwards, directors. *Roll On, Columbia: Woody Guthrie and the Bonneville Power Administration.* University of Oregon, 2000.

Penn, Arthur, director. *Alice's Restaurant.* United Artists, 1969.

ACKNOWLEDGMENTS AND PERMISSIONS

I am grateful, as ever, to those who have helped to bring my scholarship to fruition. These include Hugh Foley, an anonymous reader, and Ronald D. Cohen (to whom the book is dedicated) for reading early drafts of the manuscript and suggesting valuable improvements. My sincere thanks go to Norah Guthrie and Anna Canoni at Woody Guthrie Publications, Judy Bell at TRO-Essex, Kate Blalack at the Woody Guthrie Archives, Deana McCloud at the Woody Guthrie Center, and Kent Calder at the University of Oklahoma Press for smoothing the way so magnificently. To Bill Nelson, thank you for the maps; to Bob Land, thank you for the index and for your meticulous copyediting; and to Sean Kennedy at the Stetson Kennedy Foundation, thank you for the photo of your grandfather, Woody Guthrie's indomitable "po'folkist." To my dear life partner, my wife Judy Blazer, and my sons, Reuben and Theo, well . . . you know.

In addition to all Woody Guthrie correspondence and untitled writings copyrighted by Woody Guthrie Publications Inc., I gratefully acknowledge permission to quote from the following prose and lyric writings (all words by Woody Guthrie, © copyright Woody Guthrie Publications Inc., all rights reserved, used by permission): "1913 Massacre," "Ain't Got a Cent," "Another Man's Done Gone," "Beach Haven Race Hate," "Beluthahatchee Bill," "Big North Sea," "Black Feet," "By the Valley So Green and the Ocean So Blue," "California, California," "Christ for President," "Ellis Island Outlaw," "Get Rid of That," "Go Coney Island, Roll on the Sand," "Ice in My Whiskers," "I'm A-Goin' back to the Farm," "Keep That Oil A-Rollin'," "Let Me Join Your Army," "Lindbergh," "London City," "Ludlow Massacre," "Mermaid Avenue," "More War News," "My People," "Narrow Margin," *New Found Land*, "Ninety Mile Wind," "Notes on 'East Texas Red,'" "Open Up That Second Front

Today," "Oregon Trail," "People's Songs and Its People," "Pineytimber Blues," "Pistol Packer," "Post War Breakout," "Pretty Boy Floyd," "Racial Hate at Beach Haven," "Southern White Wombanhood," "Stetson Kennedy," "Sweety Black Girl," "Talking Sailor," *Ten of Woody Guthrie's Songs, Book One,* "The Bowery and Me," "The New York Trains," "To a Union Show Troup," "Union Air in Union Square," "Union Labor or Slave Labor," "Union's My Religion," "Voice," "War Bond Gal of Mine," *War Songs Are Work Songs,* "What Are We Waiting On?," "When I Get Home," "Why Do You Stand There in the Rain?," "World's on Fire," and "You Fascists Bound to Lose."

I am grateful for permission to quote from the following songs copyrighted by TRO-Essex/Ludlow Music (all words by Woody Guthrie, © copyright TRO-Essex/Ludlow Music, all rights reserved, used by permission): "Better World A-Comin'," "Biggest Thing that Man Has Ever Done," "Blowin' Down the Road," "Columbia's Waters," "Curly-Headed Baby," "Dust Bowl Blues," "Dust Bowl Refugee," "Dust Cain't Kill Me," "Dust Pneumonia Blues," "Einstein Theme Song," "End of My Line," "Grand Coulee Dam," "Hard Travelin'," "Hooversville," "I Ain't Got No Home," "I Don't Feel at Home on the Bowery No More," "Jackhammer Blues," "Jesus Christ," "Los Angeles New Year's Flood," "Miss Pavilichenko," "My Name Is New York," "New Found Land," "New York Town," "Pastures of Plenty," "Ramblin' Blues," "Ranger's Command," "Roll, Columbia, Roll," "Roll On, Columbia," "Seamen Three," "So Long, It's Been Good to Know Yuh," "Talking Columbia," "Talking Dust Bowl Blues," "Talkin' Subway Blues," "The Great Dust Storm (Dust Storm Disaster)," "Tom Joad," "Vigilante Man," "Washington Talkin' Blues," and "When My Good Ship Went Down (The Great Ship)."

INDEX

References to illustrations appear in italics.